WENDY KOMAC

PUBLISHING

For information on distribution rights, royalties, derivative works or licensing opportunities on behalf of this content or work, please contact the publisher at the address below or via email info@nolimitpublishinggroup.com.

COMPANIES, ORGANIZATIONS, INSTITUTIONS, AND INDUSTRY PUBLICATIONS: Quantity discounts are available on bulk purchases of this book for reselling, educational purposes, subscription incentives, gifts, sponsorship, or fundraising. Special books or book excerpts can also be created to fit specific needs such as private labeling with your logo on the cover and a message from a VIP printed inside.

No Limit Publishing Group
No Limit Enterprises
560 Carlsbad Village Drive Suite 202
Carlsbad, CA 92008
info@nolimitpublishinggroup.com (760) 544-6070

This book was printed in the United States of America

DEDICATION

For my father, Emil, who taught me the meaning of work ethic; my mother, Ann, the strongest woman I know; and my children, Lexi and Cory, who remind me every day what is really important.

My deepest gratitude to the Wendywoman team—John, Janus, Charley, Todd, Christine and Scott. Without your contributions, this journey would not have been possible.

CONTENTS

FOREWORD

SOME BASEMENT SOMEWHERE...

It wasn't just the fact that I was waking up in a damp, cold, empty basement. As an experienced alcoholic, I'd awakened in more than my fair share of strange places after all-night benders. What bothered me about this particular morning was that I didn't have a clue as to which basement this was, or where it was located.

I rolled over on my elbow, wincing as it dug into the freezing cement, and looked around. Yep—definitely a basement. There was enough exit and emergency lighting overhead to see that I was alone. The place was empty. I moved slowly to avoid turning the place into an instant carousel and sat up. Ah, there was my trusty bottle of vodka at arm's length. *Hello, friend. Oh, and it looks as if you brought a friend with you. A two-bottle night, I see. Well, that explains why I don't remember how I got here. Hmm... let's see what I do remember.*

I was working as a paralegal in a big, powerful city law firm. Actually, that's pretty irrelevant. I could have been working as a clown in a circus, a professional ice skater, or Miss America: I still would have found a reason to hate my job. I was always either changing jobs or trying to get out of my current one. I changed jobs the way most women change lingerie, usually to escape lousy co-workers—"caustic characters," as I called them.

My boss was a partner in the firm. He was an obnoxious hothead who thought everyone should cower at the sight of him, and he took sick pleasure in working all the associates to death. His management style was motivation by torture. I was the paralegal who had never gone to law school but was pretty certain I was the most brilliant person on the planet, if only the hothead would extricate his head from his butt and start listening to me. I had developed a few different coping mechanisms to handle the fact that my unique creative solutions were never heard because nobody ever listened to me. The first was my two-martini lunch, followed by polishing off the rest of the bottle later in the afternoon. Second, I immersed myself in a toxic cloud of constant frustration and bitterness. My words were not tools for communication; they were weapons of mass destruction, fired off to ensure that everyone who went near me got a taste of the personal hell in which I was living.

Our firm was in the middle of a long, two-year lawsuit with a lot of demands, time commitments, deadlines, and filings with the Supreme Court—enough stress to power the electric grid of a small island nation. Most of the time, I would stumble out of work at night, crash at the hotel next door, and drink the night away until it was time to do the same thing all over again the next day. The fact that I could expense the hotel and liquor back to the client made it a pretty sweet deal.

This basement did not look like it belonged to the hotel. Looking around the strange room and the empty bottles, I tried desperately to remember what had been different about the night before. Flashes of yelling—angry yelling, angrier than I had ever heard myself sound—filled my head. Hearing it play back in my head, I could barely associate such venom with the person I thought I was—or could be.

"How *dare* you work everyone like this! Are you trying to kill us? What kind of person are you? Nobody can live up to your expectations!"

There was more. "Why won't you ever listen to me? I have so many good ideas if only you people would listen! Why do you ignore me like this? How come you can't see what I have to offer?"

I had been screaming the same things in my head for years. The same frustrations, the same bosses, the same caustic co-workers. I wanted to unleash this on all of them. That's when it hit me. I finally had it. I had unleashed all my venom on this boss, the law partner.

In movies, once the main character releases all that pent-up anger and frustration, the sun shines through the clouds, birds start singing, a rainbow appears, and the person starts a bright new happily-ever-after life. In *my* movie, my massive purging of toxic emotions had led me into an empty, dark, cold, unfamiliar basement. Based on the story of my life, I wasn't surprised. But I was still desperately trying to recall the details of what happened between the fight with my boss and the situation where I now found myself.

That's when the terror kicked in and my breath started coming in short, pulsing gasps. I clutched my stomach and clasped a hand over my mouth. It wasn't the alcohol that was causing the waves of nausea now washing over me. Hell, I was a professional drinker. I hadn't puked from booze since I was a teenager. No, my friend vodka was not making me sick. I started examining my disheveled work clothes without really knowing what I was looking for. If I had been *raped*, would I know it? After all, the entire night from when I left the office the day before until waking up this morning was a complete blank. Anything could have happened. I felt awful and pathetic as a human being.

Since it was clear that, as usual, nobody was coming to pull me to my feet and rescue me, I dusted myself off and stood up. A hazy reflection in the steel elevator doors in front of me confirmed that I was not dead. This was no dream. I was really here, wherever here was. I didn't know how I got there, but the shapely dark haired female form in the elevator door, hobbling on one broken high heeled shoe and tucking her blouse into her skirt, still existed against all odds.

Suddenly I remembered. Damn, I had to get to work or I'd be fired! Because no matter how much I hated all my jobs and all the people I worked with, I was constantly driven by the overwhelming fear of being fired and ending up without any job at all. I had been a drifter before—for many years as a matter of fact. I hated my jobs, but I hated drifting around without any particular place to go even more. It was a completely irrational fear, and I embraced it unconsciously and wholeheartedly.

The reflection in the elevator doors got bigger as I tossed my broken shoe to the side and ran toward the elevator. Lobby! Lobby! Floor One! Something! The elevator buttons weren't lighting up. Shoot! The elevator was broken.

In torn pantyhose and no shoes, I flung open the door to the stairwell and climbed and climbed until finally I flung open the door at the top, walking into blinding sunlight. Now I was sure I was dead after all. This was that brilliant bright light you're not supposed to walk toward, right?

"Watch it!"

Nope, definitely the sun, not a mysterious white tunnel. The woman in the giant designer turtle shades who shoved me into the brick wall of the building I had just emerged from snapped me back into reality. I blinked and looked around, finally recognizing the area. How the hell did I end up on the exact other end of downtown Cleveland from where I worked? The time on the electronic clock on the bank sign across the street told me I was already late for work. By the time I could find a way back to the office, I would be ridiculously late. Fortunately, I always kept a set of clothes stashed in the office supply closet for emergencies like this.

I looked down at my hand to see where my car was parked. Every morning when I parked my car, I wrote where it was parked on my hand, so I would know where to find it later, especially after the martinis kicked in. When I moved the car after work, I would cross off the original location on my right hand and write the new location on my left. When I found my car, I would scrounge around under the floor mats to find enough money to pay the parking ticket. It was the only way out because, generally, I had no cash left. It had been deposited at the Pewter Mug Restaurant in exchange for booze. Unfortunately, all I saw on both palms were unreadable smudges of ink. But I was still determined to get to work.

Like a superhero with her cape in shreds, I hopped onto a city bus, using some coins I had begged off a passerby (an art form I had mastered from my former life) and was off like a flash into bumper-to-bumper traffic. As the bus full of workers and other outcasts like me lumbered slowly away from the mysterious office building, I briefly glimpsed the word "FUBAR" on the outside of the building. There didn't appear to be anyone coming or going out the front doors (or up from the basement). I wondered if Fubar was yet another company full of blowhards, crabby crappy characters and unappreciated genius. With a burst of toxic black fumes out its rear end, the bus turned the corner and I lost sight of Fubar.

When I finally made it to my office building, it was nearly time for my two-martini lunch. I stepped off the bus and hurried down the steps to the more familiar basement so I could take the back way up to the office supply closet and my change of clothes.

My fingernails, dressed in cracked nail polish, were just turning the knob to the emergency stairwell that led up to my all-important job when I froze—literally froze. I couldn't move a single muscle in my body. So I just stood there, one hand on the doorknob to the stairwell: to my "job security," to my two-martini lunch, to people who would never listen to me and never appreciate me, to a boss whom I fantasized about killing (just as I had fantasized about my other bosses) but hadn't because I was pretty certain a jury wouldn't buy "he's a jerk" as a justifiable defense.

I couldn't move. I was paralyzed in a sea of shit. I realized in my quest to get away from a bad job, I had become completely toxic. I knew in that moment that I was either going to have to find a new way to live, or die. Those were the only two options left. I had drunk all the rest away.

I looked through the little glass window into the stairwell. I saw the steps laid out in front of me. Suddenly I knew how to get out of the basement.

INTRODUCTION

WELCOME TO FUBAR CORP.

N ow, twenty-five years later, I am waiting outside the large double doors of a business hall, polished and prepared, standing on two unbroken high-heeled shoes. With a clear, sober head, I glance briefly at my note cards as I prepare to take the stage with a speech that I have given to countless corporate audiences, the very speech on which this book is based. As I am introduced and walk up the steps to the stage, I reflect on the life events that led me from that dark basement in downtown Cleveland into the spotlight.

I left the legal field where I worked back on that crappy, life-changing morning in the basement and got into sales. There I experienced business success as I had never known it, predominantly because I controlled what my paycheck was going to be every week. The idea that nobody would be sitting around the table at the end of the year deciding what kind of merit increase I would get was liberating. I was responsible for that. I was a five-star individual contributor.

My then husband, Tom, would constantly tease me that I would never move into management because nobody would be able to do things as well as I could, and I would have no patience for dealing with people while they came up the learning curve. Truth be told, he was right. The last thing I ever wanted was a management position. Then my paycheck would once again involve what someone else was doing or thinking, instead of just doing it myself.

But I didn't get a choice. When the management position was offered to me, I was basically given two options: Take the job, or don't let the door hit you on the way out. I did not want the job. Hell, no! I didn't want to babysit people! But having just built a new house, I *needed* the job, so I took it for all the wrong reasons. The division I had been working in had been in a morale plunge for a few years now.

Our team had floundered under the dictatorial leadership style of a new leader installed as part of a merger. After a year's worth of prayers every Sunday that our new dictator would be released to his greater good somewhere far, far away from Cleveland, he was transferred and I was left with an entire branch of walking wounded. What could I do to help all of them?

By that time, I had been using the "steps to success" I had created in my life for more than ten years. They had gotten me out of that basement. Maybe it was time to put them down on paper, give them a name, and use them as some sort of training with the team to help everyone take responsibility for his or her individual situation and get the place back on track. With no leadership training in my arsenal of weapons and nobody else in sight who had a better idea, I had nothing to lose. I had to do something and the steps seemed like a good place to start. I coined them the very original and clever "Nine Steps to Success." I wish I could tell you that there is some magical reason behind the number of the steps, but there isn't.

On Monday morning, I would give the team a pep talk that not only reviewed one step and action items but, in an effort to get them to laugh, would use my own personal blunders, past and present, to illustrate how the step worked in real life. And then a strange thing happened. The more transparent I was about how "bad" my life had been, how I had slowly and painfully crawled through broken glass for more than ten years, the more people realized, "Wow, I am not nearly as bad as she was. If she can do it, I can do it too." You never know when your story—good or bad—spoken with humility, will change someone else's life.

And so the upward spiral began, and something shocking happened from a personal standpoint. I loved winning big deals. I had always been competitive by nature. But what was even more rewarding was watching the team do things they never believed were possible. More and more, I realized there was untapped potential, unfound greatness in every one of them, and with someone by their side cheering them on, helping them execute strategy, course correct when necessary, and loving them along the way, they all turned into superstars.

The nine steps are not complicated:

1 Change your choices, and you will change your life.

2 Stop living life on autopilot.

3 *You* are your most valuable asset.

4 Do your personal best and go the extra mile.

5 Uncover the secret power of serendipity.

6 Invite discipline into your life.

7 Living your life in the exit line.

8 Power versus force.

9 Identify those caustic characters you call your friends.

It was more about action. Doing something, doing anything. As long as you started using the steps, whether it was one step a week or one step a year, your life would change. Today, I have climbed them over and over and routinely help others by teaching them how to do the same.

Before I knew it, I was taking the stage in front of business audiences across the country with my message. I've told workers across America my story in Technicolor® with all the gritty details. I told them the truth about corporate America, their leaders, each other, and themselves. My speeches also prompted me to spring into action because inevitably, after I was done speaking, people would ask me, "Where's the book?"

The inspiration for this book is my own life, a compilation of my observations and experiences of what has transpired in corporate America during the past decade.

You've seen the headlines about rising unemployment and the job searching woes of the average American worker trying to make ends meet. Therefore, the lucky ones who do have jobs must be the best batch of employees the American workforce has ever seen, right? Based on all media accounts, you would think that we finally live in a working world full of the most well adjusted, productive employees in history to date, each simply thankful to have a job to go to every day. One would naturally assume that the era of job hopping employees in an economy that allowed and encouraged it—a game of solitaire in each cubicle and incessant water cooler complaints about bad bosses—has come to an end. The workers of corporate America are simply grateful to be employed in these difficult times and are doing whatever it takes to keep their jobs, right? Have you ever heard the expression "The more things change the more they stay the same"?

It's really interesting. People who are unemployed want a job, and those people who have a job don't want the one they have. They feel overworked, underappreciated, and usually hate their boss. Ever had a bad boss? If your answer is no, hurry to the closest convenience store and buy a lottery ticket, because you are one hell of a lucky person. A recent Gallup poll of 1 million American workers revealed that the number one reason people quit their job is a bad boss. In other words, toxic leaders create leapers, and those leaping out the front door are usually the ones an organization can least afford to lose.

And for those who don't leap, a survey done in 2005 by Development Dimensions International says about one-third of workers spend twenty hours a month complaining about their rotten boss instead of doing their work. About an hour a day. Imagine what it is today! While it's true that people do stay home because of a crappy boss and absenteeism is a problem, a bigger problem is those who come to work and don't work—*presenteeism*—which costs U.S. corporations $360 billion annually as a result of lost productivity. That's Gallup's number, not mine. Based on my own personal experience as a senior executive at Fortune companies for the past twelve years, I think that number is low, although my observations are all anecdotal. Any way you look at it, when companies experience lost productivity it costs them billions, and all goods and services they produce will be more expensive for the rest of us. Bad leaders cost everyone more money every single time we buy something.

Bad leaders have a toxic touch that does more than melt money. They know how to crush corporate values and murder employee morale in a single, greed-powered blow. I've watched as new leaders (like the dictator in my previous example) come into an organization and single-handedly cause a team that was previously firing on all cylinders to implode… a near-fatal hire by the board of directors. I've asked myself over and over again what we could do to *train* those put into leadership positions to be better leaders. I finally concluded we shouldn't waste our time worrying and depending on the people put into leadership positions, but should instead worry about ourselves. Not in a selfish sort of way, but in a survival sort of way. Better yet, in a thriving sort of way.

For the majority of my career while climbing the corporate ladder, I couldn't wait to get to the Executive Suite so I could have a "real" mentor, somebody who would challenge me, stretch me, and inspire me to my next level of greatness. Tick tock went the clock as months turned into years, and with the exception of a couple of great people I met along the way, I gave up on my pursuit to find an extraordinary leader who had the time and energy to mentor me. Instead, I took my business ambitions into my own hands, creating my own game plan, my own steps to achieving my goals, dreams, and desires. After all, there was no one I trusted more than myself. *I needed to be a leader in my own life.*

And so I did just that. I became a leader in my own life. I dedicated my life to helping others do the same. I shifted my focus from my own trials and tribulations to the corporate masses who were incessantly twittering away their days complaining about their bad bosses and waiting passively for something better to come along—for someone to inspire them to be leaders in their own life. If you've worked in an office, you know the types of corporate characters I mean that seem to inhabit every company. The bossy office manager who exerts force by controlling everyone else's life; the slick sales manager who seems to have lost his heart years ago; the customer service rep who would rather tell customers "no" just to get them off her back, and the list goes on. Sound familiar?

It seemed as if everyone around me was perpetually "hanging out" in offices everywhere, waiting for that mystical elevator to success. Doors open, press the buttons, and voila, you get where you want to go without ever having to lift a finger. My steps were different. Together, they created a sturdy staircase where yes, you had to lift your feet up, make the effort, and climb, but they actually got you where you wanted to go.

During my speeches all over the United States, I share my information, basing my characters and stories on multiple real life companies that we have all read about on the front of the *Wall Street Journal*. On this particular literary journey, however, your tour guide will be "Wendywoman," a superhero of sorts, on a mission to rid corporate America of its villains and victims, or as she calls them, "crabby crappy people." Wendywoman's "flashbacks" are the real thing, pulled right from the pages of my life. Fubar Corporation, its employees, and their action are made up. Pure fiction written to make you laugh and make me feel better in the process.

The Wendywoman character is a recovering caustic character dating back to 1995. She encountered setback after setback on her journey of transformation. In the end, she emerged as an icon of courage to those who work with her and know her. Believing there is greatness in everyone, she is always searching for and finding the hidden good in all people and works as an instrument to teach them to change their choices and change their lives. She is an advocate for the people, the environment, and all those who aspire to make the world a better place.

Wendywoman works with an endless parade of crabby, crappy people at a company called Fubar Corporation. In this book, you will meet nine of them, one for each positive step toward success. The employees of Fubar know Wendywoman as "Wendy," the company's elevator operator. This group of toxic, caustic characters *loves* to take elevators. For them, the Fubar elevator represents an instant, effortless way to get from here to there and all the way to the end of the rainbow without the bother of making any effort.

Most of the time, the elevator riders aren't going anywhere in particular. They each have respective departments and floors where they *should* be working, but similar to time wasters in offices everywhere, they'd rather aimlessly drift from floor to floor causing mischief. Or perhaps they spend all their time in the elevator in search of that elusive happiness and success… a better tomorrow than their toxic today.

The exception to this rule and all the others is Wendywoman's trusted friend Tenacious Todd from the Marketing Department. You'll meet him soon.

How is this company of aimless drifters even in business? If nobody's ever where they're supposed to be and no one is ever doing any actual work, how does Fubar possibly turn a profit? Unsurprisingly, it doesn't. Each quarter's earnings are even more dismal than the last. This is a company drowning in the most toxic crap that corporate America has to offer. As you'll learn, nearly every solution that the *bored* of directors has come up with, in all its wisdom, has made conditions worse.

Fubar is a big company. It's so big that even with all the elevator rides, most of the employees have never met each other and nobody Wendywoman has ever asked seems to know what the company does. One thing she does know, from her front-row observer's seat at the elevator controls, is that if Fubar goes down, a whole lot of people are going down with it.

We begin our story on the last day of Wendywoman's yearlong mission to stop Fubar's uncontrolled plummet. Nine characters, nine floors, nine to five. It is up to our superhero Wendywoman to launch a complete turnaround. Welcome to Fubar Corp. We hope you enjoy your visit with us today. One word of advice, though: Avoid the elevator and the crabby crappies that ride it, and take the steps. They're more reliable and because you will do the work yourself, you know the work *will* get done.

GATEWAY

ENTER

ONE

http://bit.ly/AaHgjb

CHAPTER 1

THE ELEVATOR TO SUCCESS IS OUT OF ORDER: PLEASE USE THE STEPS

The elevator at Fubar was almost always on the fritz. This seriously pissed off many of the employees in its various departments. For others, it confirmed their perpetual beliefs that they didn't deserve anything better than a broken elevator in life. The exception, one cheerful, persistent fellow, was so optimistic that he believed that no matter how many times the elevator broke down, it would always start working again. This particular character went by the name of Tenacious Todd, and his faith in the elevator had everything to do with the amazing, resilient woman who operated it. In his eyes, Wendywoman was a superhero. But more on Todd later.

As we speak, our hero (and Todd's) Wendywoman was heading toward the basement of Fubar in the rapidly failing elevator. Inside the elevator cab, dressed sharply in her elevator operator's uniform, Wendywoman was not concerned about a freefall, plummet, or any other potentially life-threatening mechanical failure. It was her elevator, after all, and she had the wisdom and tools to keep it working, no matter what kind of caustic characters stuck screwdrivers in the circuits or started slicing at the cables. Whatever they could break, Wendywoman could take. She'd been where they were and knew their bag of tricks.

By the time the doors opened in the basement, Wendywoman had stripped off her elevator uniform and emerged in a plain white T-shirt, jeans, and strong, tough-soled sneakers. First, she disabled the elevator with her key and slapped an "Out of Order Please Use Steps" sign on the door, to match the other floors.

Then she stepped out into the basement, stowed her uniform in her work locker, and took out her satchel of superhero tools and weapons. She called it her "Tote of Justice." Most elevator repairmen—ahem, repair people— carried standard tools like screwdrivers, hammers, wrenches, and such. Our superhero's tools were quite interesting: an MFHD (Multi-Function Hazard Detector) that included the Venus Lie Trap, a Force Field, a Pooper Scooper, and a BS Detector with various settings to track and eliminate the corporate BS that permeates most workplaces. There was also a Golden Rope of Hope, an Immoral Compass, Executive "Shush-Up" Biscuits to instantly silence blowhard execs, and, when desperate situations required desperate actions, an Executive Weed Whacker with a flame thrower at the end. Wendywoman was well prepared to take on the caustic corporate characters on the payroll of Fubar.

Fubar is the type of company that anyone who has ever worked in an office would immediately recognize as a typical American office. It has nine working floors, if we're counting the Executive Suite—also called the Memory Loss Lounge—each home to an essential department that somehow contributes to company productivity. Wendywoman never bothered trying to work out the details of what was essential about each of those departments. She just picked up and dropped off the characters that emerged from the maze of cubicles and desks on each floor. And boy-oh-boy, what a set of characters they were!

If you've ever had the pleasure of pushing papers in a workplace, you would recognize these characters immediately. For many of you, they're the reason you call in sick when you're not, drink after work, talk your spouse's ear off about how much you hate your job and especially your co-workers, and religiously play the lottery. They're the reason you use inane phrases like "hump day" and "TGIF" as if cute nicknames speed up the quantum effect of time.

But none of that matters if our superhero can't get this damn thing to work again for the ride up the floors of Fubar! Wendywoman's mission at Fubar has a direct connection to the overall well-being and emotional stability of the workers of corporate America. She's kicking ass to make work a better tomorrow.

Wendywoman had a special relationship with the elevator. "C'mon, baby, let's do this," she muttered while strapping on her belt of "regular" tools. Climbing up her stepladder, she pushed the top ceiling panel to the side, and hoisted herself onto the roof of the elevator car with the graceful agility that can only come from a lifetime of hot yoga.

From the moment she'd first arrived at Fubar a year ago, she was the only person who could coax the elevator into action. It was as if the elevator immediately knew her touch and knew that she was the one who could detoxify the company and all the crabby crappies in it. Her MFHD even included a paging device so the elevator could call her back for repairs or in the event of trouble. Most of all, though, the elevator was her most powerful magnet for attracting and interacting with the Fubar employees and ultimately opening their eyes to the dangers they faced if they chose to remain stuck in their toxic *todays*.

The clock was ticking at Fubar Corp. Dollars were draining, pink slips were being prepared, and the financial futures of Fubar's workers hung in the balance. It was up to Wendywoman to get the elevator working and then pick up each worker according to schedule. Like most chronic procrastinators of corporate America, the Fubar characters didn't really think of the elevator as a vehicle to get from here to there. For them it was more of something to do, to pass the time, until something better came along. Have you ever had the kind of workday where five o'clock arrived and you couldn't quite put your finger on what you actually accomplished that day? That was every day at Fubar, but nobody really noticed.

For Wendywoman, the pattern of puzzled procrastination at Fubar had a strict schedule today. Nine characters, one elevator ride at sunset. But because Wendywoman was a strict believer in taking the steps instead, the sunset ride was meant to be the last time any of the characters would choose the elevator as their preferred mode of getting from here to there.

At the moment, however, her mechanical ally was in desperate need of repair. "Oh! For God's sake, not again. Poor baby," murmured Wendy over the damaged elevator.

The cables were fried, the wiring frayed from the stress of carrying toxic load after toxic load up and down the floors of Fubar. In addition to the work floors and the basement, there was also an Executive Suite on the ninth floor. Wendywoman only ferried executives to that floor where she would always be instructed to remain in the elevator because, "*You* are not allowed in there!" (as if she didn't know that by now). There was also rumored to be a roof level, a secret nirvana of sorts. When her various elevator passengers asked about that floor, Wendywoman told each one a different story, tailored to what she saw as that individual's personal nirvana. When you're an elevator operator slash repair person and your passengers are basically the only people you interact with all day, you have to make your own fun. She had a special way of dodging the question as to whether or not she had personally been to the roof level.

Our superhero replaced the fried cables with the constantly regenerative Golden Rope of Hope from her Tote of Justice. After replacing a few circuits, light bulbs, and fuses, Wendywoman dropped back down into the elevator cab, replaced the ceiling panel, and checked her work. The elevator appeared to be back in order.

"Damn fine work, if I do say so myself," she said with a smile.

After washing her hands in the corner sink, she returned to her work locker and grabbed her bagged lunch. Straddling a bench, she chowed down, contemplating the next load of passengers she had been tasked with ferrying up and down the floors of Fubar. The journey was never a straight shot from A to B. No way! With the kind of characters she dealt with, there were always bound to be dramas, distractions, and hell. She even had to break up a duel once right outside of Sales. All in a day's work as the elevator operator of Fubar.

As she ate her lunch, Wendywoman flipped open a binder and studied the profiles on her current passengers. Some of their tales were tragic, but Wendywoman was the type to find comedy where the rest of the world saw only tragedy.

"Well, isn't *she* a character. Might need a stun gun to control that mouth."

"This one just needs a good swift kick."

"Yeah, I'll give *her* some constructive criticism."

Wendywoman chuckled as she realized she had let herself slip to the dark side for a moment. Back to the mission at hand; she had to find a "nice" way of dealing with all of them. No stun gun allowed! Once her lunch was done and she had reviewed the passenger profiles one last time, Wendywoman took an invigorating shower (this basement had *everything*!) and donned her elevator operator uniform again. Her buttons and buckles all shined, pants neatly pressed, hair tucked into her uniform cap and shoes polished to a military spit-shine; she slipped on her spotless white uniform gloves, tucked her Tote of Justice into a secret compartment in the elevator, and prepared for lift off.

But just as she hit the button to close the doors, she heard footsteps outside the elevator in the stairwell leading to the basement. If she aborted now, the timing of the entire trip could be thrown off. Determined to stay on task, Wendywoman punched the "Close Doors" button on the elevator panel with even more determination.

"Hey, Wendy, wait up!" a familiar male voice called out.

She sighed with a smile and yanked out the red elevator stop handle. Mission temporarily aborted.

http://bit.ly/Afg9J6

CHAPTER 2

TENACIOUS TODD

T he elevator doors were just starting to open up again when a male arm slid between them, followed by the twinkling eyes and troublemaking grin Wendywoman had come to appreciate.

"You are trying to get me fired again!" Wendy told him, trying to sound pissed but unable to suppress a smile.

Her dear friend "Tenacious Todd," as she affectionately called him, grabbed one of her arms with the only one he had, and yanked her out of the elevator back into the basement.

"What's with the early lunch, Wendy? I know I'm not running that late," Todd teased.

Wendywoman hovered outside the elevator doors, still conspicuously aware of the big clock on the wall, loudly ticking away the precious seconds of her mission.

"You marketing guys *never* think you're running late. But then one meeting leads to another and you get wrapped up in a creative project or writing a song," Wendy teased back.

"That reminds me, I've got a *great* one I wrote last night. I think we should pull out my keyboard and—"

"Todd, I don't think you understand the seriousness of completing this mission!" Wendy exclaimed in a rare display of impatience.

Todd immediately shut his mouth respectfully and listened. He was always a good listener. He had learned to listen, really listen, to what other people were saying years before, mostly as a way of coping with the fact that people rarely listened to him. Most people—the regular run-of-the-mill, close-minded ones anyway—couldn't get past his right shoulder that didn't extend into an arm.

Todd had been playing keyboards and singing his heart out since he was 4 years old. Then, a decade later, he broke his arm playing football in the backyard. It wasn't the quarterback long bomb that snapped the fragile bone. It was cancer, and it took his shoulder and arm and almost his life.

But after enduring eighteen hard months of chemotherapy and a death sentence that most adults wouldn't have had the strength to face, Tenacious Todd hung in there and proved everyone wrong, learning to appreciate his personal circumstances for what they were. He inspired everyone around him by showing them through his actions that negative events cannot be controlled, but negative thoughts can. He learned that once you slam the door of your mind shut to negative thoughts, the windows of opportunity will open for you.

And for Todd, they did. He went back to playing keyboards (bass and treble clef with one talented, nimble hand, thank you very much), went on tour, and was even featured in a national magazine. As he moved mountains and reached goal after goal and dream after dream, Todd made a startling discovery about the "able-bodied" (ha!) folks who let an amputated shoulder and arm get in the way of seeing him as the complete, whole, and rather astonishing person that he was. There are people in the world who have *all* of their limbs and are "way" more disabled than he would ever be. Imagine that! He quickly learned there are too many people out there who are completely paralyzed by snap judgments, guilt from failing to do anything with their own lives, by creating alibis for their lives instead, and by the fear of being called on it. But amazingly enough, they're not riding around in wheelchairs. Nope. They may be emotionally handicapped, but in their small minds, they think they're fooling everyone just because they're walking around with two good arms and legs.

That's why Todd liked Wendywoman so much. She didn't need to lose a limb to see how special he was.

I'm Tenacious Todd, a smile on my face
Power of hope from a higher place
I live it to the fullest thankful every day
On a mission for others to live the same way

People, especially the crabby crappies of Fubar, tended to look at Wendywoman and Tenacious Todd the same way—as if they didn't exist. She was "just an elevator operator," there to transport their fabulous fannies from floor to floor. And he was "just that cripple," someone to be pitied but not taken seriously as a whole human being. Their friendship was a match made in heaven, so together they could survive hell.

Fortunately they didn't see it as hell. Wendy's greatest joy was finding the humor in the Fubar foibles. Todd's greatest joy in life was composing songs about the various crabby crappies that surrounded them. Wendy had a way of inspiring the lyrics in some of Todd's songs with her "gratitude exercises." When she was having a bad day dealing with Fubar's crabby crappies and the toxic atmosphere they were constantly bringing into her elevator, Wendy would force herself to say something positive—anything really—about the character in question. For instance, the company's CEO would typically spend his elevator ride to the top spewing his methane gases in her face about how the elevator was breaking down, how she never fixed it fast enough, why couldn't they have an elevator repair *man* instead of a useless woman, and such. As soon as the doors closed behind him, she would take a cleansing breath, remember gratitude, and say out loud with the utmost Zen, "I'm grateful he didn't get hit by a truck today." Hey, gratitude is gratitude! You have to start somewhere. It's never too late to change your choices and change your life. She would quickly jot down the positive comment in what she called her Book of Fubar. And man, it was a very big book.

Together, Todd and Wendy, along with her trusty Tote of Justice, shared one greatest joy in life: teaming up for Wendywoman's mission to save Fubar.

Wendy glanced at the ticking clock again and Todd noticed. As much as he enjoyed joining her on her elevator rides through Fubar, he couldn't help but remember that the first time she had invited him on board, he wasn't exactly eager to go for an elevator ride. For most of his life, as a matter of fact, Todd preferred the steps.

When he was a young boy being treated for cancer, he was allowed to wheel his IV pole containing the intravenous chemo meds around the hospital. Even though he was going through a hard time, this new freedom to escape from the terrible hospital food in his room to the basement with its vending machines full of junk food, helped him get over his previous fear of elevators. As a young kid, Todd used to watch as elevator doors closed in front of him, unsure if they'd ever open again. But during his treatments, the freedom offered by the elevators made them more into a trusted friend than a foe.

On the day he was undergoing his first chemotherapy treatment, thrilled with his freedom to move about, Todd wheeled his "chemo pole" into an elevator and set out to explore. He heard that chemo makes you violently ill, so he wanted to have a few tasty treats before the sickness kicked in. Within moments after he hit the "B" button to check out the vending machines and the elevator began its descent, it gave a massive shudder and came to a halt between floors. Panicking as any fourteen-year-old kid would in that situation, Todd started pressing buttons, banging on the doors, and yelling for help to anyone outside who might be able to hear him. He did this over and over, but nobody responded. Nobody knew where he was and he was alone in the elevator. He was also worried because the battery on his IV pump kept beeping that it needed to be charged.

Forty-five minutes later, the elevator finally moved and the doors slid open. And a few hours after that Todd's heart started beating in normal rhythm again! Nevertheless, after being released from the stuck elevator, he had no choice but to get back on the horse. After praying it wouldn't hold him hostage again, he returned to his floor so he could get the IV plugged in. Since the ride back up was without incident, Todd decided to call a truce with elevators for future rides, like the one with Wendywoman right now.

"Okay, got it. We're outta here, Wendy! Off to save the day again!" Todd hummed a superhero "and away we go" ditty and put his arm out like he was flying.

And with a push of a button, Wendy and Todd were off to their first stop. The elevator began its turtle-slow, clickety-clackety ascent to their first stop. Now you'd think, Wendywoman being a superhero and all, and having magic tools in the Tote of Justice, that her elevator would be the fastest on the planet. You would be wrong. Due to the toxic nature of its regular passengers, the elevator not only broke down a lot, but even when it was operational, it was just barely so. Todd often compared it to the elevators in the *Flintstones* cartoons, hauled up and down their stony chutes by large birds gripping ropes in their beaks. Todd was actually thinking of the *Flintstones* bird at this very minute as he broke out his best cartoon bird squawk.

"Up and down, down and up, why can't these people ever figure out where they want to go?"

Wendywoman laughed at Todd's impression. He looked over at her, beaming. He thought she had the best laugh in the whole world. Whether she was laughing at her own eccentricities and goofy missteps, laughing at his songs and imitations, or even laughing at something particularly hilarious that a Fubar employee did, her laugh was music to his ears. Speaking of music…

"So, my new song," Todd tried to tell her again. "Right now I'm calling it the *yesterday-today-tomorrow* song. It's about how you can change your *tomorrow* by making a decision *today* that is different from *yesterday*. It's a work in progress."

"Mmm, hmmm."

Wendy was watching their progress on the floor monitor above. Regular elevators showed the floor number lights flashing by as it sped from floor to floor. The Fubar elevator showed the floor numbers broken down into percentages (it took *forever* to get from one complete floor to another in the constantly ailing elevator). So, instead of seeing lit up buttons for Floors 1, 2, and 3, as you would in a regular elevator, you saw a digital floor indicator that read Floor 1.48, for instance, to indicate that you were roughly halfway between Floors 1 and 2.

The elevator also had a toxicity indicator that resembled a thermometer next to the floor indicator, with the readout showing green at the bottom and red at the top. When the elevator had absorbed as much toxicity as it could handle from all the BS and other caustic behaviors spewed forth by the passengers inside, the indicator shot right up to red. The lights at the top started flashing to warn of an impending breakdown. Nobody knew this, of course, except Wendy and Todd. She told everyone else at Fubar that it was a remote meat thermometer she was using to monitor the progress of a turkey she was cooking downstairs. On the other hand, sometimes she told them it was a heartless monitor. It didn't really matter anyway. The caustic characters at Fubar didn't listen to her any more than they did to Todd. The upside (because Wendy and Todd always found one) was that when nobody's listening to you, it can be funny to mess with them, so she constantly brainstormed new explanations for the toxicity indicator just to see if anyone ever started listening to her. They never did.

Just then, as you might expect, the toxicity indicator was at a healthy, by Fubar standards, glowing green. They had left the basement for the first floor a few minutes ago and the floor indicator showed that they were just now passing floor number 0.27.

"Wendy, are you listening?" Todd asked.

"Of course. You wrote a *yesterday-today-tomorrow* song. Tell me more."

Wendy gave Todd her full attention now.

"It's about how everyone, even the most misunderstood people, were certain people *yesterday*, which influenced who they are *today*, except most people only look at who the person is today. Their time machine of judgment is stuck in the present. Right?"

Wendy loved watching Todd talk about a new song. The sparkle in his eyes became a damn-near astronomical star explosion. She nodded enthusiastically and he continued.

"I mean people could have had the world's worst things happen to them, just awful tragedies that tore their soul apart. But heaven forbid that when you smile at them at the water cooler they don't smile back. Instant judgment! They're the worst kind of people. Case closed!"

"Exactly," Wendy agreed. "So that's your song?"

"That's how it starts, and then it goes into their *tomorrow*. That's where you come in, Wendy," he said.

"I'm in the song? Haven't you written enough songs about me, Todd?" Wendy asked.

"Never enough!"

"So do I get a preview?"

"Nope. Not yet. It's a work in progress. Plus I'm saving it for an official premiere," said Todd.

"Then you're just a big tease!" she said, playfully shoving him into the elevator railing. The elevator indicator showed floor number 0.98. They were almost at the first floor and Wendywoman's first stop of the day, when…

Beep, Beep, Beep!

Todd's pager went off. "Shoot, it's 911!"

He read the text message: "*911! Big crisis. need ur help. waiting 4 u in ur office, where r u??? –Bill.*"

They both looked up at the floor number: 0.999.

"I'll just hop off and use the steps," Todd said, as Wendy expected he would. The elevator arrived at Floor 1.0 and Todd was off and running toward the stairwell, waving at Wendy over his shoulder and shouting out his thanks. He was the only person at Fubar who ever gave his thanks to her.

With the elevator doors still open, Wendywoman now had a dilemma. This was the first stop of her mission, and Fubar's CIO Box of Rocks Bill was her first passenger of the day, but he was now up in Marketing waiting for Todd. Skipping a passenger would throw off the whole day.

Wendywoman disabled the elevator with her key, stowed her uncomfortable uniform cap and gloves, closed the doors, tossed her Tote of Justice over her shoulder, and followed Todd upstairs to Marketing to retrieve Bill. She took her work very seriously, so when her passengers didn't come to her, she went to them.

It was a long climb to the sixth floor, where the Marketing Department shared space with Sales. Wendywoman jogged up all the flights without losing her breath, thanks to years of deep breathing exercises and the constantly-failing elevator.

She kept her head down as she exited the stairwell and hustled around the outskirts of Sales. On her way past the elevator, she pressed the call button. On most elevators, the elevator would arrive in seconds. But Wendywoman knew that she had a while before the Fubar elevator made its way up five whole floors.

An obnoxious male voice shouted, "Because if you're not winning sales, you're losing customers, that's why!"

Without even looking, Wendywoman knew that Sharkman Zak was at it again, chewing out a new guy to make himself look and feel better. She shifted her Tote of Justice to her other shoulder, pondering the perfect tool to set Zak straight. But that would have to wait for later. She needed to retrieve Box of Rocks Bill first and get him in that elevator before any more precious mission time was wasted.

Only a thin partition divided Sales and Marketing, but the difference was night and day. The Sales side of the partition was loud, flooded in migraine inducing overhead lights and bustling with the illusion of activity to feed the illusion of success, each salesperson wearing his finest suit and tie to feed his own delusion of grandeur. When Wendywoman turned the corner around the partition and entered the Marketing Department, it was as if someone shut the lights off and hit the mute button.

Have you ever seen those futuristic movies where all the worker drones wear black spandex unitards with hoods that cover their heads as their supervisors whip them regularly for motivation? That was the Fubar Marketing Department. Is it any wonder that Tenacious Todd, overflowing with life, creativity, and enthusiasm was always wandering the building and riding in the elevator with Wendy? His soul was alive and kicking. His co-workers, hunched over their plain metal desks with dim light bulbs dangling overhead, while following cookie-cutter instructions to the letter, had their souls surgically removed long ago. Marketing people should be creative, autonomous, and free flowing. If you gave any of these people even one of those qualities, the paradox would drive them insane.

The worker drones were very surprised when Todd occasionally visited the department, even though he was there quite often without anyone noticing him. Most of them thought he was the assistant elevator operator. The others had decided he was a one-armed man, and that's about as far as they took any of their personal conclusions in life.

Wendywoman walked through the rows of drones, singing their worker drone song (oh-e-oh, o-eeeee-oh) in her head. Enjoying herself too much, she failed to stifle a giggle, and it came out more as a guffaw. The already quiet room became dead silent as all the marketing worker drones, all in their neatly lined up rows of desks, looked up at her with blank, dead eyes. In that split second, the same programmed computer message transmitted through each of their automated brains: *Just the elevator operator, not a real person, no further processing necessary, back to task*. As their heads went down in unison, they went back to drawing lines, all the same length and width. Selecting officially approved marketing messages and sticking them in the same place on each marketing piece, they used the same exact three colors they had always used on Fubar marketing materials, in the exact same way that they had always been used.

Wendywoman, feeling the life being sucked out of her, quickly moved on with her mission. Ducking in and out of sight of the drones, she snuck silently to Todd's office door and listened to his conversation with Box of Rocks Bill, Fubar's chief dis-information officer, a man who had less information about how to live life than anyone Wendywoman had ever met.

Most of the time, she encountered Bill on his way to or from the CEO's suite. Fubar's CEO, Methane Man, saw Bill as his greatest ally and as someone always eager to do his bidding, whether that meant spying on e-mails and ratting out employees, or simply being the CEO's eyes and ears. Wendywoman, on the other hand, was Methane Man's greatest enemy.

Her work to help Fubar's employees toward a better *tomorrow* and save the company was in direct opposition to his selfish, greedy goal of destroying it. This made Wendywoman one of Box of Rock Bill's most despised people. For that reason, she was careful to remain quiet as she listened to the conversation outside of Todd's office.

She felt and heard Todd's exasperation with Box of Rocks Bill through the door to his office. "I still don't understand why you had to page me 911 for something this simple, Bill. It's a simple task, and even if you needed help, anyone out there in the department could have helped you. Why did you call me?"

Wendywoman knew that Todd wasn't trying to antagonize Bill or belittle him. He was just seeking answers, as always, about why his Fubar co-workers acted the way they did. She was quite certain that those answers would be a long time coming. These people failed to grasp that the same level of hysteria applied to a negative situation could be applied to a future goal or objective before it actually happened. They each had the power to talk themselves into or out of almost any situation, good or bad, yet most of them chose the bad nearly every time.

Box of Rocks Bill was frustrated that Todd wasn't granting his bad attitude the respect he felt it deserved. "You can't talk to me that way! I'm the CIO! You're just... you're just... well, the marketing guy," said Box of Rocks Bill, adding defensively, "and you're never here anyway. At least I know how to do my job!"

Todd ignored Bill's little rant and remained focused on the task at hand.

"Nevertheless, here, look. I've already solved your problem. See? The sentence in your memo was missing the word 'the.' That's why it didn't make sense to you."

There was silence, which Wendywoman took to mean that Bill was peering intently at the memo in question, desperately trying to figure out which of his perfect textbooks or other nicely wrapped on-the-job training manuals failed to teach him about when to use the word "the" and in which memos. She took the extended silence to mean that he failed to figure it out.

"Well, anyway… good," Bill grumbled.

"Do you want me to take a look at the rest of the memo while you're here?" Todd offered.

Bill must have nodded because Wendywoman heard the paper change hands again. As Bill waited for Todd to complete his review, with what Bill considered Todd's "magic" understanding of words, Wendywoman continued crouching patiently outside the door, waiting for the opportunity to continue her mission.

Two worker drones passed by and saw her.

"What is the woman who presses the buttons in the elevator doing here on our floor?" Drone One asked Drone Two.

"Who cares?" Drone Two answered. They moved on.

At one point in her life, Wendywoman would have had a violent reaction to what she considered a targeted insult. She shuddered as she remembered a late night some years back in the Phoenix Sky Harbour Airport. By the end of that evening, she was certain that everyone who witnessed her outburst thought there was a psychotic woman loose in the airport.

The Phoenix heat had been stifling, making her cranky to begin with, but add a week of planes, trains, and cars, and she was worn out and wanted nothing more than to go home. The poor girl working at the EastWest Airlines counter never saw it coming.

"What do you mean I don't have a seat on this flight? I'll have you know I have a first-class seat! I'm a VIP. I have platinum status on your airline! How dare you treat me this way!" Ms. EastWest, ready to end her shift and already exhausted from her day dealing with unhappy customers, had clearly had enough, too. She fired right back.

"You may think you are a VIP, but you don't act like a VIP. You're acting like a spoiled brat, and frankly, it doesn't matter because you *still* don't have a seat. Please get out of my line."

That's when Wendy (not yet Wendywoman) spit out, "You'll be sorry you treated me this way. I'm a senior vice president and I deserve respect!"

Just the thought of those words reminded Wendy just how toxic she had once been. Ha! Deserve respect? Who deserves respect? Respect is earned. If only more people understood that. She was thankful her job title no longer defined her as a person. Her job today at Fubar doesn't represent who she is, just what she does.

In the years since, Wendy had learned that when people reach a certain level of toxicity, like the indicator in the elevator, they become broken. They are physically unable to do anything they don't normally do, see anything they've never seen, or hear anything they've never heard. Those worker drones were just two more in the ongoing Fubar parade of broken people living broken existences. The last day of Wendywoman's mission would go a lot more smoothly if she could just wrap her Golden Rope of Hope around the entire building and be done with it. But if life worked that way, therapists everywhere would be out of work. No, Wendywoman knew her mission in life required helping these caustic characters change their choices and change their lives.

She continued waiting for her first passenger of the day to emerge from Todd's office. Sure, she could have just waited in the elevator, assuming he would eventually make his way back there. But caustic characters were rather like the elevator when it hit the "red zone" of toxicity and decided to go its own way. Without clear instructions and outside their normal routines, their brains tended to cloud over with confusion, especially when they strayed from their respective departments, as Bill had on his journey upstairs to Marketing today. Yes, Wendywoman decided, crouching on the floor outside Todd's office, the only way to keep her mission on track would be to stay right here and lasso Bill on his way out the door.

"Are you sure there should be an 's' there?" Bill asked, his voice dripping with confusion.

"Why? What do you think should be there, Bill?" Todd asked.

The open-ended question was too much for Bill's closed mind. He sighed and let Todd continue to work his magic.

When Wendywoman heard Bill push his chair back and get up, she quickly retrieved her MFHD from her Tote of Justice and activated it. Lights flashed, the motor inside whirred, and the reading on the screen indicated the hazard was close, very close.

Wendywoman looked up from her crouching position and saw Box of Rocks Bill standing over her.

"What do *you* want?" he demanded angrily.

What he saw was a lowly elevator operator spying on the most important information man in the company. Box of Rocks Bill was always terrified that somebody, especially a lesser somebody, would somehow gain more knowledge and more power than he had. Fortunately, earlier that morning over a cup of coffee upstairs in the Executive Suite, Bill had done some spying of his own and learned that Wendywoman's do-gooder days were numbered. He smiled down arrogantly at the crouching elevator operator.

GATEWAY

ENTER

THREE

http://bit.ly/x65dyN

IN SUMMARY...

If Wendywoman had waited for the toxic elevator to make its way from the first floor, where she was actually supposed to retrieve Box of Rocks Bill, all the way to the sixth floor, where he had slipped away to meet with Todd, she might have misplaced him altogether. Instead, using her superhero powers of foresight and flexibility, Wendywoman gave herself permission to leave the elevator and use the steps to reach her destination faster. As Tenacious Todd always says (and sings), "When you change your choices, you change your life."

Tenacious Todd's Step to Success: Change Your Choices, Change Your Life

❖ It's never too late to change your choices and thereby change your life.

- Everyone has a shot at creating the life he or she wants, no matter what the circumstance. Make a decision *today* that is different from *yesterday*. Self-awareness is your number one priority.

❖ If you don't like your life, it's relative to the bad choices you've made.

- Have you created an "alibi" for your life? Who has been the face of the blame? Take just one bad choice you have made in the past. Peel away the layers, and gain a valuable perspective on where the responsibilities lie. Be honest.

❖ You can talk yourself into or out of almost any situation, good or bad.

- This is all about setting a positive path and attaching emotion to it. The same level of hysteria applied to a negative situation can be applied to a future goal or objective before it actually happens. Just setting the goal is not enough.

❖ Slam the door of your mind shut to negative thoughts, so that the windows of opportunity may open for you.

- Sometimes you have to know what you don't want in order to know what you do want. Negative events are uncontrollable; negative thoughts are not. In order to have complete control of your emotional state, you must give power to your feelings. Let the bad ones go.

❖ Don't neglect the journey; traveling with hope is sometimes better than the arrival at your final destination.

- Appreciate your personal circumstance. If you allow hope and fear to travel together, the journey will not fulfill you. Be grateful that you own the choices along the way.

- Happiness doesn't hide in a new house, new career, new friend, and it is not for sale. If you cannot find contentment in yourself, you will never find it elsewhere.

CHAPTER 3

BOX OF ROCKS BILL

O n that split second, being stared down at by a man-child who thought he knew everything but was incapable of changing the light bulb in his dungeon CIO computer closet downstairs, Wendywoman remembered what Todd had been saying about his new *"yesterday-today-tomorrow"* song. Wendywoman was the only person at Fubar who knew the stories of all the *yesterdays* in the building. That's why she had the most open mind there and it was her mission to open others', one closed caustic mind at a time, helping people use their *yesterdays* to propel them forward.

The stories of Fubar *yesterdays* were no secret. Wendywoman was just the only one who bothered finding out. Everyone else was too busy focused on the *today*. Wendywoman was impatient to hear Todd's song. In the meantime, she thought about Bill's *yesterday*.

Box of Rocks Bill used to rule the world. Not the real world, but rather the practice one that we all get to play in as kids before encountering the real thing. He was the straight-A perfect kid that every teacher loved to put on a pedestal as the standard by which his classmates today and tomorrow would be judged. This gave the teacher a feeling of accomplishment and the kid and his parents a feeling of something greater to come. It was win-win for everyone.

If there was a theory to be memorized and applied to standard examination testing, such as science, English or math, Bill could pass the test with flying colors. But then, as a high school senior poised to compete with the best and brightest college-bound students in the country, Bill got overconfident. His guidance counselor suggested that he branch out and enroll in AP (advanced placement) philosophy to "expand his academic horizons." Always the apple polisher eager to impress, Bill immediately obliged and dove in headfirst.

By the end of week one in class, Bill knew he was in trouble, deep trouble. There were no facts, data, formulas, or theorems to memorize and regurgitate. Philosophy involved open-ended questions where no answer was right or wrong. It was about complex arguments, ethics, and human conversations. Bill quickly realized that he was completely screwed. His perfect academic record since kindergarten was about to be flushed down the toilet. The Ivy League expectations his parents set for him by age ten were about to go up in flames. Bill needed a miracle.

And then he found one. A meek little mouse of a student named Garth who sat at the next desk looked up to Bill. Damn near worshipped him. Garth thought his seatmate was headed for the Oval Office or, at the very least, would find a new and clever way of splitting the atom. He would do anything for Bill, and that's exactly what Bill would require of him. Bill studied with Garth and was careful to copy every word of his homework assignments, as their teacher was fortunately a dimwit when it came to spotting plagiarism. At test time, Bill worked out a system to copy Garth's philosophical words. Much to his parents' complete expectations, Box of Rocks Bill passed AP philosophy and all his other courses with flying colors. The Ivy League life plan was still in play, and Bill did exactly what he was told to win the game. And win the game he did.

His Ivy League credentials were his golden parachute to a plethora of job opportunities. The world was Bill's oyster and he did exactly what his parents told him. He'd never been the conductor of his life. He was more like the guy who played second backup triangle in the percussion section if the first two triangle guys got sick.

Then Bill's parents, the only conductor he knew, died in a tragic car accident and his life was suddenly without direction. He was unceremoniously left with an Ivy League piece of paper that said he knew how to learn stuff and a few resume entries that further showed he purportedly could learn stuff in the real world versus the practice one. In most cases, he continued to get promoted to positions way above his competency and capabilities. What Bill was continually missing, however, was someone to tell him what he should do next.

Fortunately for Box of Rocks Bill, with his academic walnut of a brain strung between his ears, powered by the pieces of paper that said he knew stuff, the CEO he was currently employed by was a kindred soul. This particular windbag CEO decided that as much as Bill tended to freak out his human co workers with his exceeding lack of emotional IQ or social graces, he was pretty good when it came to computers and thus a good guy to have around. So said

CEO attached Box of Rocks Bill to his own golden parachute and the two floated from corporate gig to corporate gig, leaving a trail of methane madness in their path. Finally, they floated into Fubar. Now the methane blower was CEO, Bill was CIO, and Wendywoman was left to deal with them both.

"What do *you* want?" Box of Rocks Bill demanded of Wendywoman, who was still crouched on the floor outside Todd's office with the flashing MFHD in her hands.

Wow, thought Wendywoman, this guy really did think he was King Turd on Poop Island. Thankfully she had her Pooper Scooper ready.

"I've come to bring you back to your floor, Bill," she said, standing up on wobbly legs after crouching that whole time.

"I didn't expect to find you here," said Bill, digging for information on what she was up to.

"Yes, Bill. I've been waiting for you. The elevator is just about to arrive to take us back to the first floor," Wendywoman told him calmly, guiding him away from Todd's office while smiling at Todd over her shoulder.

As soon as she said the word "elevator," Box of Rock Bill's eyes glazed over. There was just something about the elevator that made him lose track of time, especially when it took him to the Executive Suite. He was living a shrunken little life and couldn't get out of his own way. He refused to give his life permission to expand. So, Bill kept his life restricted by doing the same things day in and day out, wearing a path in the carpet from his office to Methane Man's office to the Memory Loss Lounge.

"I don't even remember how I got here," Bill said with a dazed look in his eyes as Wendywoman guided him through the rows of marketing drones, around the partition into the den of sales wolves, and over to the elevator. Bill kind of reminded Wendywoman of herself when she would get on a conference call while she was driving to the office. She hated to admit it, but there were times she couldn't even remember which route she had taken. For the most part, she was on autopilot.

Wendywoman recognized that Bill, like many others at Fubar, was lost in a cloud of corporate toxicity and it was up to her to rescue him so that his comfort zone was off limits. The only problem would be how to separate Bill from his toxic counterpart, Methane Man, and help him realize that the gap between here, his comfort zone, and there, his renewed *tomorrow*, was not as big or scary as Bill thought. She arrived with him at the elevator just as the doors were opening.

"How did you do that?" Bill asked, still rather disoriented and looking for a procedural explanation.

"I'm the elevator operator."

They stepped into the elevator and Wendywoman put on her uniform cap and pristine white gloves again, pressing the button for the first floor where Bill the CIO lived. "Let's get you home," she said, smiling.

Still clutching his corrected memos, Bill smiled in relief. For a moment, he forgot to remember that he was far superior to the elevator operator. She was making him feel better about himself for the time being, even if he didn't know why. He forgot about all his insecurities in dealing with people, the way people would look at him when he said completely inappropriate things, and all the other pieces of life that could not be learned from the pages of a textbook or the gilded font of an advanced college degree.

When the doors closed in front of them, the floor read 6.0 and the toxicity indicator was still a solid green. It would be a long way to go, percentage by percentage, all the way down to his home on the first floor. Thankfully, that gave Wendywoman some one-on-one time to work on him. Bill stood behind her, still reviewing his memos with Todd's corrections, scratching his head.

"I just don't get it," he mused.

"What don't you get?" Wendywoman asked.

"How does he know what to correct?"

"Common sense and logic. He looks at it and just knows what isn't right," she said.

People cling to what they know so tightly, what they know they're comfortable with, and they are quick to debate their position, especially when someone suggests a different way of doing things. Bill was perfectly willing to go on believing what he had always believed and fight anyone who disagreed to the death.

"That's a bunch of crap magic as far as I'm concerned," Bill snapped. "There's no way someone can just *know* what to do! Somebody had to teach them that."

"Well, Bill, there are lots of things people know without ever being taught. Why don't you try something new and surprise yourself once in awhile?" Wendywoman suggested as the floor level read 5.65. Their slow descent toward 1.0 continued.

"What can they possibly know without being taught?" Bill demanded, closing his Box of Rocks brain to her suggestion that he throw his daily routines out the window. "Why am I listening to you anyway? You're nothing but a button pusher. What do you know?"

Wendywoman sighed, used to the piercing remarks. But after a year of dealing with this wing nut, she was losing her patience as time was running out. Determined to make herself laugh so she could stay on track, she thought about how years earlier she had heard someone recast the acronym EBITDA (earnings before interest, taxes, depreciation and amortization). In her mind, it now stood for Earnings Before IT Does Anything! Wasn't that the truth! Sometimes, getting the IT Department to do anything was like pulling impacted wisdom teeth—painful! She briefly closed her eyes for a second to rid herself of the negative thoughts when, in her head, she smiled and sung the song that Todd had written about Box of Rocks Bill.

I'm the loudest in the room, so the smartest they'll assume
That's my modus operandi
Socially brain dead, but look at all the books I've read
And my expensive tie.

"That is the problem with all you people who never bothered to get a decent education," Bill went on.

Wendywoman decided to keep her master's degree a secret for the time being. She knew it was better to let Bill have his say now and unload some of those rocks that were cluttering his walnut brain.

"Do you know that most of the problems with America could be solved if more people just got off their lazy butts and got a decent education? I mean look at our standing in the world with math and science and productivity and everything…" He trailed off, trying to remember what else that cable news story had said last night. "Look at those mindless morons we just left in Marketing. You think they have a proper education? Probably not. Who knows? I mean most of them probably can't even put a sentence together," Bill ranted, with the venom of absolute insecurity and fear in his voice.

Wendywoman noted that the toxicity indicator was on the rise from green to red.

"Have you ever started a conversation with them, Bill?" she asked him.

"With whom?"

Wendywoman sighed. He'd already forgotten where his venom had been aimed just moments ago.

"With the folks in the Marketing Department. Or the folks in any department actually. Why not welcome some change into your life and call it a good thing?" said Wendywoman.

"Are you kidding me? This is your idea of a button pusher joke, right? Every time I've ever tried to talk to anyone in this place, other than the other Ivy League executives of course, it's like I'm speaking a foreign language. They look at me with those blank, uneducated stares. I stopped trying a while ago. I mean, why would I waste my precious time, as CIO of this great company, trying to communicate with morons?"

Bill attempted what he thought was a smirk of superiority and seniority. To Wendywoman, it looked more like Box of Rocks Bill was praying desperately for a rock to climb under.

"Bill, you seem to have some strong opinions on people who aren't exactly like you," Wendywoman observed.

"Of course I do. We all do. What do you think all the executives talk about upstairs, you know, in our executive meetings? Most of this company's problems are that everyone else is too stupid to understand us!"

The toxicity indicator was now on a rapid rise toward the red zone as the elevator continued its descent to Floor 1.0. At 4.87, it began to shake and the lights flickered. Box of Rocks Bill looked like he was going to pee his pants.

"What is that? What did you do? Fix it now!" he demanded of the woman whom he considered his ultimate subordinate.

Wendywoman was already stripping off her restrictive operator's uniform down to her white T-shirt and pulling various tools from her Tote of Justice for the imminent repairs she was anticipating. Bill was staring blankly at the flashing lights on the control panel that looked nothing like the computer code he was used to.

"Bill, I think you're giving a lot of people a bad rap," Wendywoman said as she pulled off the cover of the control panel. The elevator was shaking even more, had slowed nearly to a halt, and the lights were flickering wildly. Looking at Bill's terrified face, she figured she had his full attention now.

"What? What do you mean?" Bill asked, his voice shaking at the uncertainty of the situation. Maybe he was finally starting to listen. Wendywoman could almost see the lights flickering on in his Box of Rocks brain.

"How do you know what kind of education we have Bill? Because of our jobs? And does your job really indicate what you know and what you're capable of in life?" Wendywoman started tinkering with various items in the control panel as Bill watched in awe.

"Of course it does. And where did you learn how to do that?" he asked.

"I taught myself, Bill."

Bill's sarcastic disbelieving laugh was cut short by the toxicity indicator hitting the top of the red zone. As lights flashed wildly, the elevator came to a complete halt. Fortunately, the lights stayed on. That wasn't always the case.

"Now what? What do we do? Help! Somebody help us! We're trapped in the elevator!" Bill was yelling toward the ceiling, perhaps thinking that his fellow Ivy League executives might be able to hear him.

Wendywoman continued her repairs calmly. "It just occurred to me that you've never even asked my name," she said.

"What? Why would I? What are you talking about?" Bill was still transitioning from panic mode to present time, realizing an actual human being stood in front of him asking questions.

"My name is Wendy. Welcome to my elevator."

He looked at her outstretched hand with confusion. Following basic human instinct, he shook her hand. He was finally present. Wendywoman slung her Tote of Justice over her shoulder, slid the roof panel to the side and prepared to climb.

"Where are you going, Wendy? Are you leaving me?" Bill said, getting used to the sound of her name.

"Nope, just going up here for a minute. You're fine, Bill. You're safe right there," she reassured him as she climbed.

She was pleased to see him attempt a human smile as she looked down into the elevator cab. When he wasn't looking for just a split second, Wendywoman removed the Pooper Scooper from the Tote of Justice and aimed it at Bill. She could almost see the bullshit rising off his brain in rings of vapor. It would take more applications, lots more of course, but it was a start.

As she repaired the elevator, they talked even more. But this was a whole new Bill she was having a conversation with. He had temporarily pried free his soul from his toxic buddy Methane Man and was a real person—shades of his past, perhaps. He wanted to know about her, where she came from, how she started working here. She kept the details general, as she did in all these situations. No real reason to share the intimate moments of her life, but in some ways, the two of them had a lot in common.

Wendy, too, had been a bright, articulate straight-A student. She didn't have the luxury of an Ivy League education, but because her father was the president of a travel agency, she gained a somewhat more useful form of schooling by traveling around the world from the time she was a young child. She had street smarts and had learned to survive—kind of like hand-to-hand combat for life. All the exposure to different cultures really helped mold her into who she was today: a mosaic of all her experiences, good and bad. And, oh, when it was bad, it was very very bad! Hanging out in countries with no rules when she was sixteen and wise beyond her years helped develop her penchant for martinis. She graduated from high school with an advanced degree in alcoholism, and that was how all the trouble (well, most of it) began.

Yes, brains were important. But being smart wasn't the end all, be all. After all, just look at that executive from Silverman Rachs who just got popped for insider trading. He undoubtedly was smart; he just didn't have a shred of common sense, and the word "integrity" must have been missing from his version of Webster's Dictionary. He was sadly lacking in his job to be a decent human being. The list could go on and on and on with names of his like-minded counterparts, but it was time for her to snap back to the job at hand.

Wendywoman was pleased that most of the rocks seemed to have cleared out, and Bill was now open to positive change. However, as much of a happy miracle this seemed to be, Wendywoman knew that realistically Bill still had a long way to go before he would lose the caustic qualities that were as natural to him as his daily routine, especially since she didn't have the luxury of keeping the Pooper Scooper aimed at him 24/7. This was merely the beginning. Bill would have to continue the work himself.

The Fubar elevator was working once again, and Wendywoman and Bill continued their descent to the first floor and his computer closet. Bill was very quiet, studying Wendywoman as a scientist would a rare, exotic specimen, occasionally looking around her elevator at all the numbers, lights, and even his reflection in the wall mirror as if seeing them for the first time. Wendywoman smiled contentedly and put her uniform back on.

Everything was going just fine, the toxicity indicator back to green, until they reached the fourth floor, Human Resources. The doors slid open and in walked Serendipitous Serena, somewhere far away in her rose-colored world. At the moment, she was absorbed in the bright, hypnotic screen of her intelligent phone.

"Well, if it isn't *sappy* Serena," Box of Rocks Bill muttered sarcastically under his breath, rolling his eyes.

Bill had a different perspective from Wendywoman's on the idea of "serendipity." While Serena's life often resembled a patchwork quilt of serendipitous events, each leading her to where she needed to be next, Box of Rocks Bill saw this kind of *new age* thinking as delusional and saccharin. Serendipitous Serena's life perspective was, admittedly, over the top, to the point that she saw everything—no matter how awful—as surrounded by a silver lining.

Despite her perennial haze, Serendipitous Serena's feet miraculously carried her into the elevator without the guidance of her eyes or brain, and she serenely stepped in between Wendywoman and Bill.

"Floor One please," Serena said, still not looking up.

"That's where we're headed," Wendywoman responded, and they were off again.

"Floor One? That's my department. What do you need from my department?" Bill asked Serena, confused that someone would need something from him without any advanced warning.

Still engrossed in her phone and the flickering images on the screen, Serena said, "There's something wrong with my Fakebook page. I can't tag any of my overindulgent friends in my inappropriate party photos or tag Fubar so I can reveal company secrets to our customers and competitors."

Well, that's what Box of Rocks Bill heard, anyway. Serena had actually said Facebook, but what entered Bill's head and what was processed through his box of rocks brain were different things entirely.

Even before he erupted, the toxicity indicator restarted its rapid rise from green to red. Wendywoman held onto the elevator railing, knowing what was coming.

"HOW DARE YOU BE ON THOSE DANGEROUS UNPREDICT-ABLE WEBSITES WHEN YOU KNOW THAT THEY ARE COMPLETELY UNSECURE AND AS CIO I HAVE NO CONTROL OVER THEM WHAT'S THE MATTER WITH YOU ARE YOU AS STUPID AS YOU LOOK OR EVEN DUMBER (breath) I CAN'T BELIEVE YOU PEOPLE WHAT ARE YOU TRYING TO DO TO ME DON'T YOU KNOW I'M A GENIUS SO WHEN I SAY NOT TO DO SOMETHING WHY WOULD YOU DO IT YOU STUPID USELESS WOMAN!!!!!"

Before Bill's toxic explosion even had a chance to enter the atmosphere of Serena's rose-colored world—BAM, CRASH—lights out. The elevator started its wild plummet downward. As Serena and Bill clutched each other in the dark, like scared siblings hiding under the bed as Mommy and Daddy sparred, Wendywoman calmly took her Golden Rope of Hope from her tote and wrapped it around them both. She held the rope tightly around them until, seconds later, the toxicity indicator returned to green, the lights went on, and the elevator returned to its normal slow descent. Bill and Serena didn't notice as Wendywoman removed the rope, stowing it in her tote again.

"I'll just drop you at the next floor, Serena, and you can walk back up to your floor," Wendywoman said.

Serena was still busy rebooting her emotional computer from the sudden unexpected "bad" status back to her natural state of "everything's always good." Bill stood scowling at the phone that Serena still clutched in her sweaty hand.

By the time the doors opened at Floor 3.0, Serena was smiling serenely again, and Bill was staring upward at his Ivy League colleagues floors above, no doubt wondering what they would have done in this situation. As Serena entered the stairwell for her climb back up to Human Resources, she began to sing. She'd show Bill. He apparently did not know about ShhTwitter. On ShhTwitter, she could anonymously tweet about what an idiot Bill was, and he'd never even know it was her!

When the Fubar elevator finally reached Floor 1.0, Bill wasn't that surprised to see Wendywoman lock it and follow him into his computer closet. She watched as he sat in his familiar, comfortable, ergonomic executive office chair, surrounded by his servers, oversized monitors, keyboards, and pages and pages of code taped on all the walls. There were no other seats in Box of Rock Bill's virtual kingdom, so Wendywoman stood in the doorway, arms folded as Bill started typing away.

"What do *you* want?" he demanded.

"You know my name now, Bill. There's no reason to pretend anymore," Wendywoman told him.

He turned to face her with a look of uncertainty and fear.

"What do you want, Wendy?" he asked less harshly. Wendywoman really wished she had had more time to suck the old, stagnant stuff out of Bill's brain, making room for some new thoughts, new ideas, new perspectives. After all, Bill had been thinking the same way day in and day out for years. But time wasn't on her side anymore, so she was going to have to make do with the flashes of progress she had seen earlier.

"I want you to make a decision, Bill," she said. "You've gotten a glimpse of what is possible today. You've seen how your life could be if you open your mind and start seeing people outside your Ivy League, ivory tower mentality. I think you know that people are basically good and that judging a book by its cover only leads to unhappy endings. But I think you're afraid to talk to people and find out. It doesn't have to be this way. There is a way to change. Because by the time you have figured out that your life isn't working, it will be too late. You can change your *tomorrow*."

Bill was listening, considering her comments with his new partially opened brain, thanks to the amount of poop removed in the elevator.

"How?" he asked.

"One hour before sunset today, I'm going to come back for you, and we're going to take the elevator up, picking up all the others like you on the way," she said.

"How far up?" he asked.

"The Executive Suite and then—the roof."

"But, but… you can't go up there… I mean, how can you get up there? How can any of us get up there? It's too high… we might all fall off…" he stammered.

"You'll just have to trust me, Bill. Can you do that? Will you be ready when I come to get you later?"

Bill stared at her, deciding.

http://bit.ly/xKx7ul

In Summary...

Box of Rocks Bill was just fine, even on his way to becoming a whole new person, until Serena and her phone brought him right back to his "normal" self. That's so true about making changes, especially big ones in your life, isn't it? Tons of Americans learn this every year when they make New Year's resolutions—eat right, exercise, lose weight, finish that book, learn a new skill, control stress. But then what happens? Life shows up, just like Serena's social networking habit and all those good intentions fly right out the window. If we only had a "Golden Rope of Hope" to wrap around ourselves and make everything okay again! Until then, consider breaking out of your "computer closet" with these tips and insights from Box of Rocks Bill.

Box of Rock Bill's Step: Living Life on Autopilot.

❖ Are you living a shrunken little life?

• Get out of your own way. Give your life permission to expand. We keep our lives restricted by doing the same things day in and day out. The gap between here and there is not as big as you think.

❖ Stop standing on what was, or even what is!

• Use the past to propel you forward, not to pull you back. You must understand that change is positive and part of who you are. Exercise change daily. Make your comfort zone off limits.

❖ Most of us love to cling to what we know—what we are comfortable with—and are quick to debate our position if someone suggests a different way.

• There is a tendency to go on believing what we have always believed, all the while trying to have a different life experience. This may explain your stagnant life. Throw your daily routines out the window, try something new, and surprise yourself.

❖ If it doesn't work—if it's broken—fix it! If it's not broken—fix it anyway!

• Don't trick yourself into thinking that something is working, so you shouldn't change it. By the time you have figured out that it isn't working, it will be too late. Make a habit of finding things that are working in your life, and make them better.

❖ Transformation is a constant in life, whether you want it or not. Rather than forcibly resisting the new, welcome change, and call it good.

• Take every risk and embrace every opportunity to provide a better life for yourself.

• Every day new cells are born and old cells die. Your body is constantly in a state of change. Match up your external environment and embrace the evolution. Be born into the parts of your "unlived" life.

CHAPTER 4

LAME-O LEO

F loor 1.82 en route to Accounting, Floor 2.0. Wendywoman prepared for her next stop, the next case on her mission. This caustic character felt like a two-for-one-deal. When Lame-O Leo was around people he perceived as higher up on the food chain than he was, he begged for their approval. When he was looking down at the people on the rungs below him, he would politely request approval. How did Leo end up living in this world of fear, constantly seeking validation from outside of himself that he was a worthwhile human being, because the man in the mirror simply didn't see it? Once again, Wendywoman thought about Leo's "*yesterday.*"

In a typical backyard, deep in the Midwestern suburbs, a young boy had been hard at work since sunrise, struggling to build the perfect tree house. The boy was actually afraid of heights, but he had two motivations for his special construction project. First, he wanted to make his father proud of him for doing something all by himself and working so hard. Second, he wanted to build a place where he could hide from his father.

It was almost sunset when little Leo banged in the final nail and triumphantly climbed down the ladder to look up at his work. It was a lot higher in the tree than he remembered. He wondered if he would ever find the courage to climb the ladder to the top again. His father joined him in the backyard and stood next to Leo gazing upward at the tree house.

"I woke up at dawn this morning to get started, Dad," little Leo said proudly.

"Mm-hmm," his father said, circling the tree to inspect the tree house from all angles.

"And I worked hard all day. I even skipped lunch."

"Mm-hmmm."

His father climbed the ladder in a few fearless strides and was soon inspecting Leo's masterpiece at eye level.

"When my friends came by to play I told them, 'no thank you, I have a job to do,'" Leo continued eagerly.

His father stopped short at one of the windows, took a tape measure out of his pocket, and started measuring, frowning.

"What is it, Dad?" Leo called up from the bottom of the ladder.

"This isn't right. The numbers don't add up," his father admonished.

Then he climbed down the ladder to confront his son.

"Leo, there's no point in doing something if it's not right. It's just a waste of everybody's time," his father said. Then, as he looked directly in the boy's eyes, he added, "And it makes you look like a damn fool."

Leo hung his head in shame. He spent the next three days tearing down the tree house and rebuilt it again from scratch. When his father didn't come out to inspect his work, Leo went to him, tracking him down in his study.

"I worked hard," he began, but then reconsidered his words. "I mean, I got it right this time, Dad. Want to come out and see?"

His father didn't even bother looking up from the book he was reading.

"Nope. If you say you got it right, then you must have got it right."

That was the end of that. Leo learned that day always to get it right and never expect any praise. But that didn't stop his inner "little Leo" from continually seeking it. Now an adult, Leo continued to seek someone else's approval, practically begging those around him to tell him he did a good job.

Leo, like so many of us, failed to see the invisible labels and lies that his father and subsequent others had taken upon themselves to stick all over his neatly pressed suits to keep him steeped in what he couldn't be, wouldn't be. Wendywoman wanted to see him peel off and discard all those labels, clean out his closet of lies about who he currently was and could be, and reveal the truth: that *he* was his most valuable asset. Not his damn car or house, but Leo himself.

Wendywoman arrived on Floor 2.0 and made her way through the tapping of calculator keys and scratching of pencils on paper in the Fubar Accounting

Department. In unison, the sounds made up their own symphony, and Wendy-woman started humming along as she made her way back to Leo's office. Not one number cruncher paid her any mind.

When she arrived at Leo's office, however, it wasn't Leo she found. She collided with his boss, the CFO, Not Me Lee, a man who thought everyone else should do all the things he didn't want to. He was looking guilty and in a rush as he left.

"Lee, what are you doing down here?" Wendywoman asked him.

"I wasn't doing anything," Lee mumbled, pushing by Wendywoman and speed-walking toward the stairwell in the corner like a rat abandoning the *Titanic*.

Wendywoman would deal with him later. Right now she was becoming increasingly irritated that none of her pickups were where they were supposed to be today. Unlike many of the others, Leo had actually requested an elevator ride up to the CEO's suite. When Wendywoman first got this request, via her MFHD, she was sure it was a misprint. Leo wanted to go *up* in the elevator? Wendywoman knew how terrified of heights he was.

Her last harrowing account with Leo had been when the elevator had gone on the fritz when he was a passenger, sending them on a white knuckle, rapid trajectory toward the top of the building. When they reached the roof, level R on the floor indicator, the doors remained closed, and Leo became suddenly curious.

"What's out there? I want to see," Leo said.

"Not yet, Leo. Maybe someday though," Wendywoman told him, smiling at this unexpected glimpse of courage.

Then, the elevator dropped, and Leo grabbed the elevator railing in breathless terror again, forgetting his curiosity about what was beyond the doors on the roof. And now he wanted to go up again? Wendywoman was instantly concerned that something was wrong.

This only contributed to Wendywoman's ominous feeling that the final piece of today's mission, at sunset, was not going to go smoothly. On the other hand, at Fubar, when did anything go smoothly? And in the end, that was okay. Because life was never a straight shot from point A to point B, but instead, it was a road filled with detours and sometimes potholes that you had to learn to maneuver through if you wanted to be successful.

She was just scribbling a note for Leo, letting him know she had been here to pick him up, when he walked in the office. He had been standing in the men's bathroom down the hall staring in the mirror and washing his hands, trying to cleanse his mind of all the toxic thoughts. He stared and stared, trying to figure out why he couldn't just get one person on the planet to tell him he did a good job, no matter how hard he tried. He stared harder and harder until he felt invisible. That's when he finally left the men's room and ran into Wendywoman in his office. He immediately felt better about himself. At least he wasn't just an elevator operator.

"You called for an elevator, Leo?" she asked him.

"Yes. Let's go."

He grabbed a leather-bound file of papers and led the way to Wendy-woman's elevator. As he walked through the rows of his paper-pushing subordinates, he tried to emit an air of superiority, to show them that he was on a critical assignment.

"Well, the reason I called for the elevator," Leo said, speaking louder than necessary since Wendywoman was right behind him, "is that I have a very important meeting with the CEO" —emphasizing C-E-O even louder—"about very important matters."

Leo pretended not to notice that not a single pencil pusher looked up or even appeared to have heard him. He stopped short at the elevator, rifling importantly through his papers while he waited for Wendywoman to open the doors.

Once inside, with the toxicity indicator still green, Wendywoman and Leo began their ascent from Floor 2.0 to the CEO's office on Floor 8.0.

"So, you have an important meeting with the CEO?" Wendywoman asked kindly, to show she had been listening.

This time Leo squirmed uncomfortably as a shadow of dread crossed his face. "Yes, yes. Well, there are some purchase orders that somehow got all fubar'd, and I've been called to straighten the whole thing out."

"Wow, that's impressive Leo, that the CEO himself would call you for such an important problem," Wendywoman said.

Leo looked at her for the first time and straightened up, growing a full inch in that elevator and actually smiling. "Well, yes, I guess I am an important person. I'm glad you noticed that," he said.

"'I'm glad you noticed that—Wendy.' My name is Wendy. Welcome to my elevator," she said extending her hand.

Leo gave her a loose-gripped, limp-wristed shake, then quickly retracted his hand and started rifling through papers again. "It's the darndest thing actually," he said, still rifling. "I could have sworn those purchase orders were right, completely and 100% right, when they left my desk. I can't imagine what he found wrong with them."

Wendywoman suddenly flashed back to her collision earlier with Not Me Lee as he left Leo's office. She sighed, realizing how her day was getting more complicated by the moment.

The elevator let out a little shimmy. The toxicity indicator was just barely above green, so Wendywoman wasn't concerned. But Leo jumped and grabbed onto the railing with one hand, gripping his file with the other, looking as if the building was crashing down on them.

"What was that? Are we falling?" Leo asked breathlessly.

"No, not at all. What are you…" Wendywoman stopped short and saw that Leo was ghostly white, absolutely terrified. She laid her hand gently on his arm.

"What's the matter, Leo? Are you okay?" she asked with concern.

"I'm… I'm… I'm a little scared of heights," Leo confessed. "You see, I had this tree house when I was little…" As Leo told Wendywoman the tree house story, she realized that this meeting with the CEO was like confronting his father, who, similarly, never gave him praise for anything, no matter how "right" it was. Leo had spent his whole life waiting for his father, his teachers, and now his boss to invest in him, rather than making the choice to invest in himself.

"Wow, Leo, I'm really sorry to hear that. But I'm sure your meeting with the CEO will be just fine," Wendywoman reassured him.

Suddenly Leo got angry, lashing out at her. "Just fine, just fine, just fine! What is it with the women in this building and everything always being just fine? You're like that dingbat in HR!"

"Okay, it probably won't be just fine at all. Is that better? What do you want me to say to help you face this, Leo?" Wendywoman asked.

"How about an ego boost? How about telling me what a great accountant I am and that none of this can possibly be my fault? How about that?" he demanded.

"Leo, one thing I've learned in life is that you can't always depend on getting a pat on the back from someone else. You have to learn how to say these things to yourself. If you can't believe in yourself, why should anyone else? If you wait for someone else to tell you that *you* are your most valuable asset, you might as well just ride this elevator forever," Wendywoman told him.

"What do you know? You're just an…" Leo started as all the others usually did.

"Elevator operator. I know," Wendywoman sighed. "But do you honestly think that's all I've ever been?" Leo scratched his head. He'd never thought about it.

While Leo thought about it, Wendy was remembering the late 1990s when she worked at Paperclips, Inc. Her evil boss, Tim Moss, caused her so much stress that she found herself in the hospital with seven ulcers— convinced there was one for each letter of his name. He gave new meaning to using words as weapons. He would rather die and burn in hell than give her or anyone else who worked there a compliment. She couldn't take it anymore! She was in danger of growing ulcers on her ulcers from worrying about why he refused to acknowledge her achievements.

And then it hit her. If she didn't find a way to pat herself on the back, she would die waiting for him or anyone else to do it. She laughed to herself as she thought of the photocopy of her hand that she had taped to the wall in her office. Deciding that it was not Tim's responsibility to tell her she did a good job, upon deciding she was worthy of it, she pressed her back up against that photocopy and gave herself a pat on the back.

Whenever someone asked about the hand on her wall, she would tell that person, "I can't get a pat on the back from anyone else, so I give myself one." Before you knew it, hands were springing up all over the Paperclips, Inc., office!

Yes, Tim Moss was a worthy adversary for Wendy. But, in typical Wendy fashion, she had found a way to respect Tim (even if it was just for a minute a day) even though she didn't really like him. Little by little, their relationship went through a transformation, and now, when Tim was in Chicago on business, Wendy and Tim often had dinner together and reminisced about old times. Many of the employees from Paperclips, Inc. who knew Tim, found it hard to believe that Wendy was actually friends with Tim, after enduring years of hardship under his leadership (like that time he threw golf balls at people in the sales meeting to "get their attention"). But Wendy was happy with the way things had played out. She tried consistently to focus on something positive about Tim and, in return, it seemed that those positive attributes started to show up in their relationship. A win-win for both of them. Lost in her memories, she forgot for a moment that she was still holding the mirror she had taken out of her Tote of Justice. She had wanted to share it with Leo for some time now.

"What's this?" Leo asked Wendywoman.

She'd just handed him the mirror, but he could tell it was no ordinary mirror. "I want you to see what I see when I look at you. This is you, Leo. Here, look into it," she said, placing it in his hand.

Leo did, and what he saw wasn't anything like what he saw in the men's room in accounting. The man in this mirror was smiling, confident, standing tall, and sure of his accomplishments. Here was a man who was a leader in his own life and lived it on his terms.

"Look familiar?" Wendywoman asked him.

Leo squinted a little and brought the mirror closer to his face. In those brief moments that Leo was studying himself, Wendywoman remembered how it had felt when she finally realized that the reflection in her own mirror was significantly different from what other people thought or saw in her. That day was when she discovered that she was her most valuable asset and traded in the image of the drunken loser for a woman who was confident and believed in herself. It had been a long time ago, but she remembered it as if it were yesterday.

"Looks like me, but different," he said.

"Leo, this was you when we first entered the elevator a few minutes ago. Remember? You felt proud that the CEO personally requested *you* to solve an important problem," Wendywoman said.

"Yes, but weren't you really the one who was saying that and I was just agreeing? And then I told you the truth—that I'm meeting with the CEO because I somehow messed up. I didn't do something right." Feeling shame, Leo tried to move the mirror away, but Wendywoman kept it in front of him.

"Leo, I want you to hold onto that first moment now. Forget about the rest. Focus on that moment when you were giving yourself a pat on the back for a job well done. Focus hard on that."

As Wendywoman said that and Leo focused on his reflection, the mirror began to glow with energy. Leo was so focused on focusing that he didn't notice. As the mirror glowed brighter, so did the expression on Leo's face. He felt stronger and stronger, his self worth energized by his brand new mirror. The smile on Leo's face grew so wide and so fast that the muscles in his face felt like they would crack from years of inactivity.

Zzztttttt!

The power surge in the elevator nearly threw Wendywoman off balance (thank goodness again for the yoga). Leo was oblivious, staring so intently and passionately at his reflection in the magic mirror that he didn't notice the jolt. He also didn't see what the power surge did to his magic mirror. It was glowing at maximum capacity. He felt more powerful, almighty, fearless, and freakin' invincible than ever before! He was ready to scale tall buildings in a single bound! He was ready to fly! He was ready to take on the CEO! Then, Leo had a better idea. He knew *exactly* how he wanted to put his new superhero super-confidence to good use.

As Wendywoman frantically worked to repair the damage caused by the power surge, Leo planted his feet in the middle of the elevator, slapped his hands on his hips, tossed the file aside, and spoke in a mighty booming voice.

"Wendy! I have decided *not* to go to floor number eight for my CEO meeting. No, Wendy, right now I *must* visit floor number seven to handle much more urgent matters!"

Wendywoman's jaw dropped. She knew exactly what Leo had in mind and she knew it was a terrible idea. But none of the tools in her Tote of Justice had ever backfired this badly before, so all she could do was send the elevator to the seventh floor and hope for the best.

Leo was now speaking to his reflection in the mirror. "That's right! Not only am I just going to do right things in my life, I'm going to do them faster, better and more often. What am I waiting for?" he exclaimed to himself.

The elevator doors had barely finished opening on Floor 7.0 before Leo was out like a shot, running down the long, barren hall on the empty floor with only one office, one employee—the office manager, Maniacal Mean Marsha.

"Wait! Leo! You forgot your…" Wendywoman frantically yelled down the hall.

But he was through the office door marked with Marsha's name in giant lettering before she could catch him. Wendywoman looked down at the mirror in her hand and realized that it wasn't glowing anymore at all. The power surge had apparently short circuited all its energy. She also realized that she'd forgotten to teach Leo how to recharge it. Now that it was officially his mirror, she was powerless to give it energy. When in need of a power boost, he would have to do it himself.

"That may be true," thought Wendy, "but I can still keep him from getting eaten alive." She dashed out of the elevator, forgetting to lock it behind her. She was nearly at Marsha's office door when she heard someone exit the stairwell behind her.

"Todd! What are you doing here?" Wendy asked, momentarily forgetting what was happening behind the office door.

"My, oh my, lady, you're just never where you're supposed to be today, are you?" he teased.

"Tell me about it! Hey, I'm glad you're here. I may need your help. Let's go!" Wendy grabbed Todd's hand (and smiled at the reason to do so) and together they entered the Fubar fortress of the company's own wicked witch.

"Oh noooo," moaned Wendy. "We're too late."

Lame-O Leo and Maniacal Mean Marsha's working relationship added new meaning to workplace hostility. Wendywoman would have called Marsha a workplace bully, but at Fubar there were so many of them at the executive level. She was just one of many. At the same time, Todd began to sing the jingle he had written about Marsha just to get Wendy to smile.

> *That Marsha's so maniacal and is the queen of mean*
> *When I hear her stomping footsteps, I hide to not be seen*
> *Down my throat she shoves advice*
> *And not once has it ever, ever been nice*
> *Always putting me down*
> *Turns my smiles to frowns*

The confident, super-powered man in the mirror from just a few minutes ago was once again a whimpering, pleading, shell of a man, cowering on the floor at the feet of Maniacal Mean Marsha. As Lame-O Leo begged for mercy, Marsha, a large woman with menacing eyes, her lip curled in a continuous sneer, her overly made-up face contorted in an expression of loathing, continued showering him with her word daggers.

"Loser! Pathetic! Wimp! You'll never be anything! How *dare* you challenge me? You piece of worthless filth!" Marsha sneered, arms folded above him, thoroughly enjoying herself.

"Oh! Now, Marsha, haven't we talked about this before?" asked Todd diplomatically.

Marsha slowly lifted her head and redirected her sneer at Todd. He stood in front of her desk, eyes sparkling and charming grin intact, which just pissed her off more. Marsha's daggers were powerless against Todd's sense of self worth and comfort in his own skin.

"Well, if it isn't the loser lovebirds!" she sneered.

"Oh!" Wendy realized she was still holding Todd's hand and quickly dropped it, but not before Todd smiled and winked at her.

"Marsha, why are you wasting your time on poor Leo here? In the long run, this isn't going to help you feel better about yourself. So why bother?" Todd reasoned with her.

"What do you know? You're a cripple, and your girlfriend pushes buttons in an elevator. You're both worthless," Marsha fired back.

Once again, her word daggers bounced back on her. Seeing she had no effect, she turned back to continue her assault on Leo. But Wendywoman and Tenacious Todd were too quick for her.

"Oh no you don't!" exclaimed Wendywoman. She and Todd swooped in, picked up what was left of Leo, and rescued him from Marsha's clutches.

As they left, Wendywoman called back over her shoulder, "I'll be back, Marsha. I'll deal with *you* later!"

Todd and Wendywoman helped Leo back down the hallway toward the elevator. With his eyes partly rolled back into his head, he kept moaning the same thing over and over. "I'm not afraid, I'm not afraid, I'm not afraid…"

"That's great, Leo. Good for you. Now let's get you back to your office," Wendywoman said reassuringly.

"No, have to go to the CEO… have to defend myself… my responsibility to save myself," stammered Leo.

Wendywoman was once again amazed when she realized that with a little bit of mentoring and loving, Leo had already started his transformation.

"Hey, our ride's here," Leo mumbled, still recovering from Marsha's word daggers, as the three arrived at the end of the hallway.

"Shall we?" Wendywoman said, motioning toward the elevator.

"Nah, you know me, Wendy. I prefer the steps. But thanks!" Todd said. "See you later!"

"Bye, Todd, and thank you!" she shouted back.

Back in the elevator, back on their original journey to the CEO's office on Floor 8.0 (at Leo's insistence to "finish the job"), Wendywoman handed the formerly very Lame-O (now much less Lame-O) Leo his magic mirror and taught him how to use it. She explained that change wouldn't be instant, and he would have to work on it every day to truly become the Leo in the mirror in real life. There were many things Leo was not, but the one thing Wendywoman saw in him that gave her hope for the leader she knew he ultimately could be, was the right moral fiber. He had the "personal" core values to move up the ranks and make a difference at Fubar. Maybe not today; but someday, if and when she ever got this sewer hole of a company cleaned up, Fubar could use a man like Leo. She completed her instructions about the mirror with one last piece of advice.

"Don't use it in thunderstorms or too close to power outlets, okay? Because next time Marsha might eat you for dinner! Oh, and one more thing. The mirror will not last forever. At some point, you are going to have to learn to sustain the results of the mirror without it. You'll know when that time comes."

Wendywoman and Leo laughed. The floor indicator flashed 7.95. They were close. Leo started to look nervous again.

"What is it?" Wendywoman asked him.

"I was just thinking about the tree house again. This kind of seems like climbing it all over again, hoping it's right," he said nervously.

"Except this time, Leo, you know it is. And you also know that even when it's not, you are smart enough and good enough at your job to fix it," Wendywoman told him. Then she explained her final elevator run of the day to the roof at sunset.

"Sunset?" Leo asked. "That's when…"

"I know what all this reminds you of, Leo. That's why it's important that you are in your office when I pick you up later. Can you promise me that?" Wendywoman asked.

"I'll think about it," he said.

When he left her elevator and headed toward the CEO's office, Leo was smiling. Wendywoman smiled, too, as the doors closed in front of her. She was headed back down to retrieve the next character. But if she had stuck around up there on Floor 8.0, here's what she would have seen: *As Leo strode with renewed confidence toward the CEO's office, past the empty secretary's desk (smoke break), through the stench of rotten leadership that constantly permeated the office, he heard voices behind the door—the voices of the CEO and Leo's boss, Not Me Lee, the CFO. What Leo heard horrified him.*

GATEWAY

http://bit.ly/z8MDM8

IN SUMMARY...

So all it took to put some wind beneath Lame-O Leo's broken wings was some words of encouragement that reminded him, Yes, *you* are an important person, you *do* deserve great things, and you *are* doing an awesome job. Well, that and a magical mirror that rapidly amplified these revelations. But be careful when engaging in such accelerated self-help programs. As Leo learned, it's easy to get carried away and find yourself in situations you are not yet prepared to handle. Here are some more lessons to be learned from Lame-O Leo's step to success.

Lame-O Leo's Step: *You* are your most valuable asset

❖ Invest in yourself by believing in yourself.

  • Don't wait for a boss, a teacher, or someone else to invest in you. The only person signed up for that job in this lifetime is you. If you can't believe in yourself, why should anyone else?

  • If you depend on things outside of yourself to supply you with joy, you will be doomed to disappointment.

❖ Peel off and discard any labels others have felt compelled to stick on you.

  • Is your wardrobe filled with labels and lies that others have taken upon themselves to give to you? If so, it's time to clean out your closet and reveal the truth. Only you know who you are.

❖ Never listen to anyone who tells you what you can't and shouldn't do.

  • How do they know? They are not you. Heeding their advice will only result in disappointment. Be the leader in your own life.

❖ You are on your own in this world—it's your responsibility to save yourself.

- No one will throw you a life preserver; you must learn to swim. Avoid scenarios that create judgment and self-doubt. It is your job to release others from this responsibility. Life is for living on your terms, not theirs.

❖ Don't just do the right things for your life—do them faster, better, and more often.

- What are you waiting for?

CHAPTER 5

NOT ME LEE

W hen we last saw Fubar's caustic CFO, Not Me Lee, he was in the CEO's office on Floor 8.0 having a conversation that was clearly disturbing to Lame-O Leo, who was just outside the office door. Wendywoman had dropped Leo off for his scheduled meeting with Methane Man, Fubar's toxic, gas spewing CEO. Leo had spent the better part of the week scratching his head until he had nearly created a bald spot, trying to figure out how those purchase orders had gotten mysteriously fubar'd en route from his desk to the CEO's when he knew he had done them correctly. When he arrived for his meeting and accidentally overheard the conversation between Methane Man and Not Me Lee, an extremely distressed Leo finally got his answer and stopped scratching his head.

Meanwhile, back at the elevator, Wendywoman had her white-gloved finger on the button for Floor 3.0, ready to go pick up Not Me Lee in his CFO office. She, of course, didn't know that he was already on Floor 8.0, since she had just dropped Leo off without lingering. Call it elevator operator's intuition or the fact that so far today, not *one* caustic character had been at the right pickup location at the right time, but Wendywoman suddenly decided to lock the elevator, grab her Tote of Justice, and find out exactly where Lee was at the moment.

Outside the frosted glass double doors of the CEO's suite, Wendywoman powered up her BS Detector and set it on *track* (indicated by a little diagram of the boogeyman being chased down by Wendywoman in her super cool red suit and red boots). And track it did, showing Lee's blinking red dot right behind the door of the CEO's office.

However, as Wendywoman started to open the solid-gold door handles of the CEO's office—*Whoosh!*—a flash of chocolate brown corduroy clutching a file and making odd whimpering noises burst through the doors and she had to leap to the side to avoid being trampled.

"Leo! Slow down! What's the…" Before Wendywoman could get a complete sentence out, the stairwell door had slammed behind Leo and she heard his frantic footsteps carrying him back to the safety of his little office. Another problem to deal with later, she thought.

Breathing through her mouth to avoid the executive stink, Wendywoman entered Methane Man's office looking for answers as well as Not Me Lee, who she had a sneaking suspicion had to do with the former. The source of the stink and the source of Leo's problem was emerging from the CEO's office. The two men were shaking hands, patting each other on the back and basking in their chief executive superiority to every other living thing. Wendywoman checked her BS Detector and was grateful that it was set on *track* (as in track down the caustic character who's full of it) and not *eliminate* (as in eliminate the "it"). The way these two were basking in it, if the detector had been set to eliminate, the energy generated may have short circuited the entire city block.

"Well, Lee, I want to thank you for bringing this matter to my attention," Methane Man spewed in a hearty tone of voice.

Wendywoman nearly passed out from the fresh stench unleashed in the room.

"My pleasure, my pleasure, sir. Just want to make sure my people are held totally accountable for doing their personal best—no excuses," Lee lied through his teeth.

Here was a guy, thought Wendywoman, who had set his own personal bar of accountability so low that he was constantly clunking his head on it and forgetting everything from how he ended up working at Fubar and what he was supposed to be doing there, to why the Fubar funds kept disappearing without a trace. Lee had squandered countless opportunities to prove that he could do his job, especially in situations when it meant putting in a little extra effort. He failed to see that he would never reach great heights of success if he only performed at high levels when others were watching (like his revered boss Methane Man).

Methane Man was eating up Lee's BS with a giant spoon. Lee was nodding his head "yes" to everything that Methane Man was saying. Wendywoman knew that Todd would be unhappy with her for what she was thinking next, but she couldn't help it. She was so sick and tired of Lee being the *&#@$%* "yes-man" to Methane Man just to suck up to him. With his eyes wide and a big fake smile plastered across his face, his head bobbed up and down and up and down. It made her want to hurl.

"That's why you're my number two, Lee. You're one of the only people I can trust around here."

"Number two is right," she thought. Bleh! But what the CEO said next made Wendywoman feel even sicker.

"I'll get that paperwork down to HR right away to terminate Leo."

"What?" The word escaped from Wendywoman's lips before she could stop it. Both men looked over at her, standing in the doorway, noticing her for the first time.

"What do *you* want?" Methane Man sneered.

He didn't exactly know how big of a threat she was, but something about this elevator operator got under his skin. She was up to no good. He couldn't prove it yet, but he knew it just the same, despite the fact that she was supposedly just the loser elevator operator. This chick was up to something. After all, she had been to see both Bill and Marsha today. What did she know?

Even though everyone in the place knew he was a rat, his reputation with the board had been pristine, or so he thought. Had someone finally gotten to the board and told them how big a rat he really was? Did his team know what was going on? He had intentionally disbanded that Internal Audit and Compliance Department when he first arrived at Fubar. He didn't need those spies looking at everything he was doing. In the meantime, his facial expression said it all. He didn't trust Wendywoman for a second.

Ha, thought Wendy. What a joke! If that wasn't the pot calling the kettle black, as if he knew what the word "trust" actually meant!

"He," Wendywoman said, gesturing toward Lee (but not with the gesture she wanted to use), "called for an elevator." Lee nodded and followed her to the elevator. He had a habit of losing his way. A side effect from years of having his head stuck in the sand.

"I'll get that paperwork taken care of," Methane Man repeated with a wave, disappearing back into his office, wondering why Not Me Lee would call for an elevator. Was Lee conspiring with the enemy? Methane Man had been wondering about this for some time. Executive loyalty was important to him—especially if his evil plans were to be successful today. What did she want with Lee? She needed to go, and she needed to go now. He felt his power and control being threatened and was willing to do anything to maintain it.

Wendywoman switched the setting on her BS Detector from *track* to *eliminate* as she and Lee entered the elevator. "Back to your office?" she asked him.

"Um, hmmm, sure," said Lee, distractedly typing into a pocket calculator.

Wendywoman suddenly remembered an argument she'd once had with Not Me Lee about the numbers on the digital floor indicator in the elevator. He had tried to issue her an "executive order" to round the floor numbers from the hundredth decimal point to the tenth. He had it in his head that the reason for Fubar's unexplainable financial woes was an accounting system that was intentionally set up to be confusing. Lee became very angry when Wendywoman refused to reprogram the floor indicator as he wished and stormed out of the elevator. He had made the choice that day to dislike Wendywoman without getting all the facts, making a quick judgment call based on her status and that one conversation.

They began the long descent from Floor 8.0 to the CFO's office on Floor 3.0. Since the low setting wasn't eliciting the results she wanted, Wendywoman cranked up the *eliminate* function on her BS Detector to the next level to see if she could sift through the shit and get to some real answers. She loved all the tools she had developed over the years to keep things on track in her life.

"The numbers just never add up," Lee mumbled, hitting the keys on his calculator even harder, as if ordering them to make sense. He was a prime example of why corporate America was currently dying a slow death. He was constantly poking holes in Fubar's financial books, contributing to the slow leak that was gradually destroying the company and everyone in it. The story of Lee's life would be titled *Where Did All the Money Go?* But for everything Lee didn't remember, there was one thing he always did remember: when in doubt, leave someone else to hold the bag and take the blame. It was unfortunate that Leo from accounting was in the wrong place at the wrong time today. Lee had been using Leo as his own personal garbage disposal for years now.

Just then, Wendywoman saw the toxicity indicator on the elevator start to shoot up. She looked over at Lee, still punching numbers into his calculator, but she could tell his mind was elsewhere. Maybe the BS Detector was working after all.

"Lee?" she asked to get his attention.

"Well, it's his own fault, isn't it? I wouldn't have had to keep stealing that loser's work if he had just stood up for himself and demanded credit for his own work!" Lee exclaimed angrily, bringing the conversation he'd been having with himself in his head out into the open.

"Is that how you really feel about what you did, Lee?" Wendywoman asked, moving behind him so she could crank her BS Detector up and aim it directly at his head.

"Of course," Lee said defensively—reflexively. He whipped around to look at her so fast that Wendywoman barely had time to hide her detector. "It's none of your business anyway. What do you know? You're just a…," Lee started as all the other ones usually did.

Wendywoman extended her hand. "Hello. I'm Wendy. Pleased to meet you."

And just like the others, that's when Lee saw for the first time that there was an actual person in the elevator operator's uniform. As the elevator passed Floor 6.13, Wendywoman chatted with Lee, trying to bring him back to the subject of Leo to purge his soul and ready him for the sunset ride later that day.

But no matter how she tried, and no matter how much she cranked up her BS Detector/Eliminator, Lee continued to punch numbers angrily into his calculator, thinking about whose work he was going to steal next and take credit for so he wouldn't have to do anything himself. In the meantime, Wendywoman's mind drifted back to a moment in her career that had been a turning point for her.

Early in her sales career, Wendy had known what it was like to want to make it to the top and to be willing to do just about anything to get there. She'd never stolen anyone else's work and claimed it as her own, but there had been that time when she was working at Morton's Food Service Company where she took the idea of "doing her personal best" to a somewhat toxic level. Sometimes too much of a good thing can actually be bad for you. As one of only three women among a sales team of three hundred selling institutional food, she wanted nothing more than to be the number one rep invited to join the exclusive Platinum Club of winners. Every quarter, Morton's offered several contests for the salespeople to participate in. And Wendy had been out to win them all. In her quest to achieve that Platinum Club status, her analytical brain figured out something no one else had ever figured out in the history of the company: the algorithm the company used to calculate the quarterly contest results. With that knowledge in hand, she started winning. And winning. And winning.

Eager to want to make her branch better, she shared her knowledge with her teammates. And pretty soon they were winning. And winning. And winning. It wasn't exactly cheating—as if there are really degrees of cheating. She had convinced herself that it was more like beating the system, until the system decided to beat her. During her annual review, which she had thought would go flawlessly, her boss instead asked for her laptop and her company car keys. She was out of a job! Yes, she'd made it to the top, but there were plenty of big, bad mistakes on that climb.

For a while, she pointed fingers at anyone and everyone she could, blaming them for the fact that she was now unemployed. Then, it finally dawned on her. She had done it to herself. She had let her own personal core values, the very foundation of her life since she had sobered up nine years earlier, get twisted in her goal to reach the top. She had tricked herself into thinking it was "okay" to manipulate the contests. After all, she was working her ass off for Morton's. The company should appreciate all her efforts, even if she was a prima donna, right? Not! Morton's had done her a big favor when, as a company, it stood by *its* core values and made sure everyone saw what happens when an employee breaches them. Cheating would not be tolerated. Wendy was too young and stupid at the time to see the real value of Morton's, how it invested in its people and was the leader in innovation in a somewhat less than innovative industry.

It took her years to figure out that Morton's, more than any other company, had contributed to her success as a leader on a number of different levels, including the lessons around core values and the fact that you either have integrity or you don't. Now she constantly reminded herself how grateful she was that she had worked at such a innovative company. Based on the way her career had progressed, it now seemed that it had been a once in a lifetime opportunity, unless she could get this train wreck at Fubar cleaned up.

Wendywoman shared some words of wisdom with Lee, in hopes of catching him off guard and breaking down the barrier. She told him that when you allow detours and potholes to deter you from reaching your goals and refuse to go the extra mile to get where you need to go, the only person you hurt is yourself. That extra mile is not for the company, not for your boss. Going the extra mile is for you. It is the investment you make in you, since you are your most valuable asset. Wendywoman explained to Lee that mediocrity in the workplace only creates insecurity and almost certainly guarantees that you'll be among the first to be downsized. But her words bounced off Not Me Lee's hardened shell of mediocrity and false sense of confidence that Methane Man would never betray him.

Wendywoman sighed. The BS Detector was cranked at full power, but Lee refused to give up the goods. That's when she decided to pull out the heavy artillery and unleash the Venus Lie Trap from the MFHD. To Wendywoman's delight, the instant she activated the lie trap, it started working. Lee put his calculator away and stared intently in space, as if remembering something he had wanted to tell her for a long time. She gave him her undivided attention and prepared to trap all Lee's lies about Leo and all the rest of his Fubar fibs and mathematical missteps. But to Wendywoman's shock, that's not at all what she got.

When Wendywoman's Venus Lie Trap opened its jaws, what it got in return was the reason that Not Me Lee was living his life of maximum mediocrity and excuses, deaf and blind to everything that was going on around him. Wendywoman knew that everyone had a *yesterday*, just as she had hers, but Lee's *yesterday* was one of the few remaining at Fubar that she hadn't learned about before.

Politics is a dangerous game, especially when you work in the biggest gladiator arena of them all, D.C. When hungry, eager young people with their steely eyes fixated on one elusive White House start clawing their way up to the top, things can spin out of control quickly. Yes, being an intern in Washington can truly test what a young person is made of.

Not Me Lee had been one of those hardworking, eager-to-amaze interns, struggling to impress the former movie star in the Oval Office who had inspired him to be a better Lee every single day. Forget work life balance. Lee was the first one at his desk in the morning, the last one to leave at night and had no concept of what phrases like "personal life" and "weekend" meant. Lee was always the first intern the higher-ups called for important tasks, especially tasks that required long, grueling hours.

That was exactly what happened one sweltering August afternoon nearly halfway through the first term. Polls were down and tension was up, and throughout the capital, many interns were looking for a way to get by and survive without breaking a sweat. Lee was different. The heat, the stress, the hours, and the competition—nothing had fazed his energy or work ethic in the least. He was still firing on all eight cylinders, just as he had on day one.

So, of course, Lee scored the big project that turned out (much to his competitors' dismay afterwards) to mean big brownie points for whichever intern completed it successfully. Lee did more than that. He kicked that project's butt all the way back to his alma mater, Stanford, where hard work was all it took to succeed. This time would be different. Lee had learned that in the real world, especially the warped world of Washington, DC, hard work meant nothing if someone else found a way to stomp on your head on his way up the ladder.

That August, Lee had watched in dismay as his lazier, less talented and surprisingly more manipulative competitor took credit and was handsomely rewarded for Lee's work. The blood drained from his face. How could this have happened? His *yesterday* was defined. He had gone the extra mile. He had done his absolute personal best. He had worked mercilessly to make his boss and team look good, just as he had been raised to do. Not because someone was watching, not because someone told him to, but because it was the right thing to do. And for what? What was the point? From that second on, Lee had known in his broken heart that nothing was worth fighting that hard for, if only to be stabbed in the back. This lesson was subsequently and bitterly reinforced every time Lee saw his former competitor, now a U.S. senator, on television. And judging by the senator's reputation, he hadn't changed any of his wicked ways, yet kept getting reelected every time. That clinched it for Lee. Why go the extra mile when you can just carjack someone else on the way?

At Floor 4.90 the toxicity indicator was holding steady, part red and part green. Wendywoman knew that Not Me Lee, by reflecting honestly on the details of his *yesterday*, was as open as he would ever be to embracing a new *tomorrow*. She saw this over and over at Fubar. *Yesterday* they were damaged, *today* they're toxic, and *tomorrow* they can change.

"Lee, I want to talk to you about my last elevator run of the day today…"

But before Wendywoman could finish her special sunset invite, Lee cut her off, glaring at her in an unusually toxic way (for this point in the elevator ride anyway). "Operator…, Whiny, Mandy, whatever your name is—why are we going down? I don't belong there. I belong upstairs in the Executive Suite with the others!" said Lee.

"But you said you wanted to go down to your office," said Wendywoman.

"Stupid woman, what do you know? You didn't hear me right. I said exec-u-tive suite!"

Wendywoman looked down at her Venus Lie Trap to see if it had backfired and was spitting out lies rather than collecting them. It appeared to be in working order, but Lee did not. He was all puffed up now, with no thoughts of fretting over his calculator or worrying why the numbers weren't adding up, not feeling guilty for throwing his inferiors under the bus. It was as if his trip back into his *yesterday*, when the world was his oyster and he was willing to work as hard as it took to earn the pearl, had created a super-thick shield of bullshit that every weapon in the Tote of Justice was completely powerless to penetrate.

Wendywoman sighed and changed the elevator's direction, sending it back up toward the Executive Suite on Floor 9.0 rather than to Lee's office on Floor 3.0. She realized why he suddenly wanted to go upstairs. The memories of his *yesterday* and the person he had been before he got burned were too overwhelming. Wendywoman called the Executive Suite the "Memory Loss Lounge" for a reason. Executives often wanted to go there to get a quick, powerful infusion of "I Am Awesome" juice to forget their transgressions, forget how many heads they'd stomped on as they climbed up the corporate ladder, and congratulate one another on being kings of their universe.

The elevator arrived at Floor 9.0 with the toxicity indicator in the red zone. The doors opened to the Executive Suite, the biggest double doors Wendywoman had ever seen. Their blank, imposing façade offered nothing warm or inviting, not even a potted plant nearby for decoration, as that might have given the subordinates, the outsiders, a taste of the life beyond. This was corporate America at its most pompous.

"*You're* not allowed inside." Not Me Lee smirked, as if Wendywoman were somehow oblivious to this. "But I am. I've always been allowed here."

"I know you have," Wendywoman said, motioning for him to leave the elevator, while simultaneously squashing her urge to kick him out of it. Still smirking, Lee entered the Memory Loss Lounge to forget all the things he didn't wish to remember.

Wendywoman was about to take the elevator back to the basement for repairs when… "Shoot! I almost forgot!" Hurriedly locking the elevator, Wendywoman bolted through the forbidden doors of the Executive Suite after Not Me Lee.

GATEWAY

ENTER

SIX

http://bit.ly/A7nIoT

IN SUMMARY...

Darn it! Once again, just when it appeared to Wendywoman that she was making progress and helping yet another caustic character see the light, that person slid back to those old, comfortable, toxic ways. When Not Me Lee opened up to her in such great detail about his *yesterday* and the pain and betrayal it had caused him, Wendywoman was sure he was on the road to *tomorrow*. Of course, she had been sure with Lame-O Leo, too, and look what happened to him: he had been crushed into a fine powder by Not Me Lee. This was the toughest batch of caustic characters yet, and Wendywoman was sure it would take a miracle to get even one of them up to the roof by sunset.

Not Me Lee's Step: Always Go the Extra Mile

❖ Who's watching you?

- You will never reach great heights of success if you perform at high levels only when others are watching you.

- Sometimes, when it is not your job to do it, it is a once-in-a-lifetime opportunity to prove that you can.

- Participation and cooperation over and above what's expected create enduring power, whereas forced participation and cooperation will end in failure.

❖ Always do your personal best.

- Only you know what that is.

- Learn to dismiss your tendency to believe first impressions or make quick judgment calls. Liking or disliking someone is a choice. Don't make that choice until you have all the facts. You never know if what you are experiencing is an individual's personal best at that moment in that circumstance.

❖ Work to your highest standards.

- Attitude + Quality of Service + Quantity of Service = The Job You Hold. Excel in all three, and the promotions will take care of themselves.

- If you want the shackles to fall off, throw yourself into your work with enthusiasm and with initiative.

❖ Don't get caught up in the cycle of trying to figure out why somebody did something or questioning a particular circumstance.

- The path that speeds us toward our dreams and desires is filled with detours and potholes.

❖ To the degree that you go the extra mile, your life can be equally fulfilling and satisfying.

- If you don't, the only person you will hurt is yourself.

- Mediocrity in the workplace creates insecurity: going the extra mile doesn't guarantee that you won't be downsized, but being mediocre certainly does (at some point).

CHAPTER 6

SERENDIPITOUS SERENA

The doors opened to reveal sparkling marble floors covered by luxurious Oriental rugs, with the finest imported leather furniture in the world. Banks of windows spanned from floor to ceiling, but these always appeared slightly smudged, so you couldn't really tell what you were looking at. Fubar had spared no expense in creating the most lavish Executive Suite possible, so that when its executives traveled up to the Floor 9.0, they could immerse themselves in the reflections of their egos, while forgetting exactly how they got there.

Despite the most hard-and-fast rule at Fubar about subordinates entering the suite, Wendywoman walked through the room freely with no need to conceal herself. She was surrounded by the equivalent of dementia patients at a nursing home, except this was corporate dementia! When a caustic character with executive power walked through those same doors, it was as if that person's memories of all bad deeds done were wiped clean. Wendywoman looked around at the blank, contented stares in the Memory Loss Lounge and found the person she was looking for over by the window. Not Me Lee was admiring the muddy view without seeing it.

Wendywoman sighed. It was too late to have the conversation with Lee she'd meant to have in the elevator about the sunset elevator ride. She would have to wait until he left the lounge and returned to the Fubar world again. But while she was there… hmmm. Wendywoman caught a glimpse of a plain, wooden, comfortably worn door in the corner of the suite, almost hidden behind a potted plant where the executive amnesiacs would never notice. A plastic sign tacked to the door said simply "President."

Wendywoman turned the imperfect, paint stained doorknob of the door and took in the view. It was the elusive office of the president of Fubar Corp. She looked around and nodded her head in approval. The president's office was not what most people would expect and seemed to be a direct contradiction to the rest of the Fubar executive offices. This office looked as though it belonged to someone who was, well, approachable. It had design, intention, and sophistication, but at the same time it demonstrated importance. A beautiful picture of an angel hung on the wall and the faint sound of babbling water moved through a fountain in the corner. Ahh, serenity. Since walking into the office, Wendy realized she felt calmer. The atmosphere was soothing and inviting. Her energy, which had begun to wane, was being restored, almost magically.

Buzz!

The vibrations from Wendywoman's MFHD told her it was time to stop exploring and get back to her ailing elevator. By the time she exited the Executive Suite through its large gilded doors and entered the elevator, the toxicity indicator was flashing bright red. She would need to get the elevator back to the basement for repairs, and fast! Wendywoman was usually calm about her elevator's constant need for repairs due to the constant presence of toxic characters. But she had never been this high up in the building with the indicator flashing maxed out before. The situation was dicey, to say the least.

With a silent prayer, Wendywoman hit the basement button. Her next charge, Serendipitous Serena on Floor 4.0, would have to wait. Floor 8.90, 8.73, 8.42… She held her breath and crossed her fingers as the elevator made its slow descent. At Floor 8.0, the elevator stopped completely, and Wendywoman sighed in resignation. At least the lights were still on, the engine still whirring, and the toxicity indicator still flashing. When the doors opened, she knew that the elevator had not broken completely—yet. It had been summoned by the only person at Fubar besides her who had the power to do so.

Immersed in his usual cloud of execu-stench, CEO Methane Man hurriedly entered the elevator clutching some papers. Wendywoman knew immediately what they were. "Operator! Get me to Human Resources. I have some very important papers to deliver this instant!" he said breathlessly, overwhelmed with excitement at the prospect of firing an employee.

Wendywoman knew she had to prevent Leo's termination papers from reaching Serena in HR, but she was in no position to do this now. If Methane Man wanted the elevator to go down to Floor 4.0, it was her responsibility to push that button. But not surprisingly, as soon as she did, the elevator died. The doors immediately opened, but the toxicity indicator, lights, motor, and buttons fell dark and silent. Methane Man's toxicity, in addition to everything else the elevator had endured today, had simply overwhelmed it.

After covering Wendywoman with a brief explosion of verbal excrement, the CEO made his version of a mad dash for the stairwell, wheezing and sweating from the toxic sludge that clogged his veins.

Wendywoman knew she had to intercept those papers before they got to Serena's desk in HR. Thinking quickly, she whipped the Golden Rope of Hope from her Tote of Justice, lifted the bottom floorboard out of the elevator, fastened the rope securely and strapped her Tote of Justice to her waist. Then she held on tight and slid down the rope to Floor 4.0, Human Resources.

"Wheeee!" She enjoyed every moment of the wild ride down. She was used to it. It was kind of a metaphor for her life. She swung out onto Floor 4.0 to thwart Methane Man's dastardly plan to fire Lame-O Leo. Arggg, just as he was finally becoming de-lame-ified! With no sign or smell of the Fubar CEO, Wendywoman raced into Serena's office, passing a line of employees outside that included Lame-O Leo, Box of Rocks Bill, and Maniacal Mean Marsha.

"Hey, no cuts!" Marsha yelled.

Wendywoman ignored her and rushed into Serena's office, closing the door and interrupting Serena's meeting with... nobody. As usual, Serena was hunched over her intelligent phone, tap-tap-tapping away. Serena heard Wendywoman come in but didn't look up. "Just a sec, I need to finish posting something on the fence," Serena mumbled.

"About whom?" Wendywoman asked, trying to catch the HR manager off balance. She succeeded.

"Zak just left. He was telling me about one of his sales guys who was cheating on his wife." Serena's head jerked up. She saw Wendywoman and registered a brief expression of panic on her face before smiling serenely again through her rose colored glasses. "But that's fine, right? I'm sure everything will turn out just fine."

I'm Serendipitous Serena
In my happy world of pretend
My denial keeps me standing here
Keeps me stranded here
I stay numb most of the time
But if you ask, I'm always fine

Wendywoman sighed, knowing it would take far too long to explain to Serena why dishing dirt on other people, just to unburden your own conscience, was far from "fine."

This was only one toxic aspect of the most cheerful, happy, unburdened employee at Fubar, who was also the dysfunctional soul at the heart of the company. Serena had built up a very unhealthy psychological immunity to the fact that yes, bad shit does happen to good people, and life is indeed a series of problems. Most of us find ourselves either in one now, just coming out of one, or getting ready to embark on another at any given time. Serena refused to see that. Her rose colored glasses had lenses thick enough to be windows in the Space Shuttle.

Watching Serena cheerfully violate Fubar's "code of ethics" for all the online world to see, Wendywoman found herself flooded with words of wisdom that she desperately wanted to share. For instance: "Don't allow outside forces (like the ones who influenced Serena on how to be unethical in the first place) to prompt bad behavior in your life. See yourself as the initiator of your actions." But first she had to deal with a broken elevator and a CEO who was on his way to cut one of her caustic characters loose before she could escort him, and all the others, to their elevator ride at sunset.

"Oh, is my elevator here?" Serena briefly zoned back in and noticed Wendywoman standing there again.

"Unfortunately, no, it's not. The elevator to the top is currently broken. Can I interest you in the steps?" said Wendywoman.

"What do you mean, broken?" Serena asked in confusion.

Wendywoman smiled in understanding. Of course, Serendipitous Serena would have no idea what the word "broken" meant. After all, she herself had been "broken" for several years now. It all started on Serena's first day at Fubar, when she was a fresh faced Pollyanna, right out of college with her human resources degree, ready to take on the world. If there was a corporate wrong, she was determined to right it. If there was a bad seed, she was certain she could flush that person right out the front door with the power of her optimism and expert human resource skills.

On her first joyous, innocent day in her new job as assistant to the assistant of the senior VP of HR at Fubar, Serena had just come back from lunch and stopped by her supervisor's office to find out if there were any new projects where she could be of service. She knocked lightly and then, without being invited in, opened the door, in accordance with her world view that professional people were always seated at their desks, doing their work diligently and with nothing but the highest order of work and personal ethics.

Throwing open the door with a big smile and ready-to-work attitude, Serena's world view shattered like a glass tower, into millions of tiny, sharp shards and fragments. These were the very shards of glass that Serena would willingly and blindly walk through from this moment on at Fubar. Her supervisor was neither sitting at her desk nor working diligently to ensure the success of the company. Rather than sitting at the desk she was laying on it, and the only success she was ensuring were the unseemly acts that the VP of HR was currently performing on her. In utter denial of what was happening, Serena made up a good reason for it in her mind (perhaps her boss had thrown her back out and the VP was helping her onto a flat surface) and fled the scene.

Later that afternoon, Serena, still shaken but still not completely stirred by what she had walked into, was on her way to a companywide meeting. The CEO had called it so the same VP of HR could roll out the new "Fubar Core Values System" that each person would be required to swear allegiance to. As the VP went on and on about the "integrity," "honesty," "ethics," and "accountability" that Serena so fervently believed in, she sat smiling contentedly, nodding her head in agreement with everything her boss was saying. By this point, she had pretty much revised the memory of his misdeeds as an innocent misinterpretation on her part.

Then it came time for everyone in the company to stand and place their right hand on the leather bound collection of core values that had been passed down each row. Like military recruits vowing to defend their country, all the Fubar employees rose to their feet and, with solemn faces and hushed tones, vowed to defend the company's stated core values. Serena suddenly heard the words she was saying. She heard them loudly, as if they were being broadcast over the speakers at a rock concert. *Integrity*! I will defend. *Honesty*! I will defend. *Ethics*! I will defend. *Accountability*! I will defend. She could no longer deny what she had seen. In fact, the sounds, smells, and images of what she had walked into filled every corner of her mind and threatened to suffocate her. The conflict was more than her Pollyanna worldview could handle. She was drowning, dying, and then something short circuited in Serena's brain. Then there was… nothing. Her eyes glazed over and her arms went limp. A brand new, rather creepy, smile spread across Serena's face. Pollyanna had become Serendipitous, and in the most Stepford Wives of ways.

Ever since that moment, Serena had been wading through a sea of broken glass, with the mental inability to see the blood pouring from her feet or the steam coming out of the ears of those around her. The more she said, "It's fine," the more they wanted to strangle her. As toxic as her Fubar co-workers were, they were still well aware that everything was not fine.

"*Hey*! Elevator operator! I said *no* cutting!"

Wendywoman was jarred from her reverie by the appearance in the doorway of Maniacal Mean Marsha and all the others who had been waiting their turn for their weekly griping sessions to Serena (during which she would tell them each, "Everything's fine," even if they told her the building was on fire). Wendywoman found herself bodily tossed from Serena's office headfirst by the crabby crappies that had been waiting in line.

Woozy from her unceremonious and painful altercation, Wendy remembered a time in her life when something really bad had happened to her and, unlike Serena, she had faced it head on. Even though Wendy's mom was really great, as Wendy's life got busier with her own children and her career, she was spending less time with her mom. It wasn't that she didn't love her; she just ran out of hours.

Wendy had been in Kansas City one bright, summer day, getting ready to give a keynote breakfast speech. Her mom had been at home in Cleveland. While mentally preparing for her speech, Wendy observed her phone, set on silent, light up three times. Restricted. Restricted. Restricted. She looked at her watch. Only twelve minutes before she was supposed to start. Normally she would ignore it, but intuition told her "listen to the messages."

"Wendy, this is Metro Hospital Life-Flight. Your mother, Ann, was hit by a truck during her morning walk."

In the background, Wendy could hear emphatic voices: "Ann! Ann! Ann, stay with us! Ann! Ann, stay with us. Ann! Ann, we're leaving Wendy a message. Is there anything you want to say to Wendy?" Wendy heard her mother's voice, weak and wavering, say, "Tell Wendy I love her."

In that moment the only thing Wendy could think of was, "If my mother is saying 'tell Wendy I love her'—something she doesn't say very often—she's dying."

Wendy hadn't had much time to think about it or to react. Her assistant told her that it would be several hours before she could get a flight to Cleveland, so Wendy decided to go ahead and present the speech as planned to the several hundred people or so who had gathered, then leave immediately afterward. But as she looked out over the crowd to begin, her heart sank. In that moment, she realized her mom had never seen her present her inspirational speech. Hell, her mom didn't even really know or understand what it was that Wendy did for a living. Now, she might *never* know.

Wendy's mom had been walking the same route for more than thirty years. Five miles a day, same route, same time. On that day, she didn't know why, she walked an hour later. She had even taken a slightly different route, turning one street earlier than usual, which led to a intersection that she normally wouldn't have crossed. She'd had her headphones on to block the sound of rush-hour traffic, so she hadn't heard the truck accelerating into the turn. Ann took a full hit on her right side from the Ford F-250 pickup, which caught her in such a way that she was propelled into the air. She had flown about ten feet before landing on the top of her head, then the side of her face, then finally on the same side of her body that had taken the impact of the truck. Under no circumstances should she have survived. People her age have been known to trip on the stairs, hit their heads, and die.

Wendy got the first flight back to Cleveland around lunchtime. At the hospital, she saw an all-but-unrecognizable woman in a bed with her mother's name on it; a woman fighting for her life in a way that Wendy would never, in her wildest dreams, have imagined or thought possible.

Ann survived her first brain surgery, but the night before she was ready to go home, the doctors announced that she would need a second brain surgery. Wendy could still hear the screams of anguish her mother let out. She and her brother, Scott, gave their mother full permission to close her eyes and go to sleep forever. It would be okay. They couldn't bear to see her suffer anymore. Their mom wanted nothing to do with that. She fought.

Wendy's mother had not realized, when she stepped out of her house that morning, how close she would be to the number one spot in the exit line. Her life changed second by second, block by block during that walk. She could have ended up anywhere else if she had made different choices at any point that morning.

But the story changed from calamity to serendipity when she constantly reminded herself, along with the support of her children, that it had been an accident. The driver of the truck didn't wake up that morning and decide he was going to run Ann over in the crosswalk.

Serendipity!

At her first opportunity, Wendy took a speaking engagement in Cleveland. Her mother came and sat in the fifth row, listening to her daughter discuss her steps to success. When Wendy got to the secret power of serendipity—finding the power of good, the seed of equivalent benefit, in a seemingly tragic (or adverse) situation—her mom had no idea that the step was dedicated to her. When Wendy began the story about her mom's accident, no one in the audience was aware that her mother had survived. As Wendy recounted the story, they all seemed certain it was not going to have a happy ending.

As Wendy turned to her right and gestured to her mom to stand, the place erupted with cheers. This was a life changing moment for both mother and daughter, who had each faced something bad, head-on and together, without running for the elevators or taking the easy way out. Together they learned living their lives does not mean ignoring difficult or painful situations, but acknowledging and learning from them. That includes forgiving ourselves, forgiving those we believe contributed to the situation, and then letting it go. Wendy was pretty sure that Serena would have been running to hide at the point of impact. Forget dealing with the trauma.

Back to the present in the HR office, Wendywoman looked up from where she was lying on the floor to find Serena standing over her, looking down with a curious but contented smile. "Well, if there's no elevator, I have to get back to my employee feedback meetings," Serena said sweetly.

Wendywoman lifted her head, rubbing her bump. Through her blurred vision she saw that the caustic characters of Fubar had returned to standing in line outside of Serena's office. Leo was there to complain about Lee, Bill to complain to Serena (ironically) about the anonymous nasty tweets someone was posting about him, and Marsha to complain about everyone else. Wendywoman briefly wondered who could be inside with Serena if everyone else was out here.

Wendywoman gingerly stood up, just about ready to throw in the towel, something she *never* did. She'd been at this corporate fix-up business for more than a decade now, but this was her toughest batch yet. If they didn't want to change their choices, how could she be expected to help them change their lives, specifically their *tomorrows*?

Slam!

The heavy door to the stairwell slammed shut behind Methane Man as the sweatier, smellier, and more-winded-than-ever CEO burst into HR with Leo's termination papers in a death grip in his sweaty hand. He was apparently determined to feel the joy of ruining some poor sap's life today.

Wendywoman tried to keep her balance as the CEO swept by and headed for Serena's office door, knocking over the others in his path. With their heads obediently hanging down, nobody dared call him a line cutter.

"Stop!" Wendywoman whimpered feebly, still trying to get the fight back into her system so she could finish this challenging day. It was almost over. Wendywoman had never lost a passenger yet, and now Lame-O Leo was about to be tossed out into the street on his Lame-O butt!

But then the door to Serena's office opened. Wendywoman almost cried at the ray of hope who was shining through the door, saving her day yet again. Tenacious Todd had his arm slung over Methane Man's shoulders and was using his power of tenacious charm to send the CEO on an entirely different goose chase.

"So you say that people who aren't allowed up there are *sneaking* into the Executive Suite? This is an outrage!" Methane Man sputtered.

"It is, and I think you need to get up there and fix the situation immediately," Todd said amiably.

Seeing the opportunity to feed his evil soul by terminating a whole group of people versus just the one, Methane Man tossed Leo's termination papers to the side for the time being and headed for the elevator.

"You—elevator girl! Take me to the Executive Suite. But remember, *you're* not allowed in," the CEO ordered at a still-dazed Wendy.

"The elevator is broken. *Remember?*" Wendywoman had just about had it with these people.

The crabby crappies chimed in, supporting their boss. "You incompetent blah blah blah," they all barked and whined.

Wendywoman thought about fleeing the scene but remembered her very own words of advice: the same external event can be viewed, responded to, and judged differently based upon your perspective. Or as Winston Churchill put it, "When going through hell, keep going." So she did.

Grabbing her Tote of Justice from the floor, she pulled a lever on her MFHD, and out popped a red, white and blue package of Executive Shush-Up Biscuits, specifically designed for the CEO (seedy flavored). They came in a sleeve, similar to those instant biscuits you pop in the oven. With almost perfect precision, Wendywoman tossed a biscuit into Methane Man's big mouth, where it immediately started to expand. The CEO instantly shut up and, with bulging chipmunk cheeks, stared at everyone in the HR lobby in confusion. The crabby crappies in line outside Serena's office continued to hang their heads in subservience and Serena was back to tap-tap-tapping on her phone again.

"I think you should take the stairs to deal with the situation in the Executive Suite," Todd offered helpfully. The CEO nodded in utter confusion and disappeared back into the stairwell pulling at the gobs of gook stuck in his mouth. Once he was gone, Wendywoman stared at Todd incredulously.

"How did you know?" she asked.

"Leo told me about the whole thing in the break room earlier. I put two and two together and knew that someone would have to get down here pronto to run interference," said Todd, beaming. Wendy stared at him with kind of a silly, schoolgirl smile plastered on her face. "Hey, I think that's probably what Leo is telling Serena about right now," Todd continued, gesturing towards the office.

"Oh, I'm sure everything will work out just fine," Serena cooed to the distressed accountant. Her voice drifted sweetly out into the lobby since the door was ajar.

Leo's frantic voice carried even louder. "Fine? What do you mean? How can it be fine? What?" Leo was desperately trying to make sense of the HR airhead's complete failure to grasp the seriousness of the situation.

In the lobby, Wendywoman smirked. *Yeah, right.* Everything would be just fine, when all the Fubar problems were being solved by a faceless elevator operator and her one-armed invisible friend, both masters at changing direction rapidly and coming up with different, creative ways of responding to challenges. Speaking of challenges… "The elevator! Oh shit, I almost forgot!"

"Wendy… tsk, tsk, tsk," Todd reprimanded her for her potty mouth.

Wendy rolled her eyes at him as she headed up the stairs. "Thanks again, Todd. I'll see you later!"

Todd smiled and waved, calling his good-byes as usual, and turned to leave. He was completely surprised when she raced back down the steps, grabbed him, and planted a big, toe-curling kiss right on his lips. Wow! That made him smile even more.

GATEWAY

ENTER

SEVEN

http://bit.ly/zT8nhV

IN SUMMARY...

Well well well! Has Wendywoman lost her mind or found true love? And what about Serendipitous Serena? Will she remain in her catatonic *today* forever because she is unwilling or unable to free herself from her traumatic *yesterday*, when all her beliefs about people were simultaneously shattered?

If only Serena would realize that yes, bad stuff does happen, and it doesn't help to hide behind rose-colored glasses and pretend everything's "fine." If you don't eventually confront problems and figure out a way to move through them, you'll find yourself walking on broken glass forever.

Serendipitous Serena's Step: Secret Power of Serendipity

❖ Yes, crappy things happen to good people.

- Life is a series of problems. You are either in one now, just coming out of one, or getting ready to embark on another.

- Our job is not to ignore difficult or painful situations, but to acknowledge them, learn from them, forgive ourselves for getting into them, forgive those we believe contributed to them, and then release them.

❖ How we think and respond can be more dangerous than any adversity we face.

- The greatest challenge in life is to control the process of our thinking.

- Don't allow outside forces to initiate action in your life. See yourself as the initiator of direct action.

❖ Train yourself from this moment on to appreciate and find happiness in the simplest of situations.

• Start small and change the fabric of your thinking. This will manifest itself in all situations.

• Change direction rapidly and come up with different, creative ways of responding to challenges.

❖ The path is never clear.

• Your view of the world will have a strong influence on your actions.

• The same external event can be viewed, reacted to, and judged differently from a different perspective.

• In the words of Winston Churchill, "When going through hell, keep going."

❖ Life is the perfect teacher.

CHAPTER 7

PHRANTIC PHOEBE

F*wap, fwap, fwap.* The stairwell echoed with the sounds of Wendywoman's tennis sneakers lightly slapping each step on her way back up to the eighth floor to repair the elevator that remained dark and broken outside of Methane Man's CEO suite. She had changed clothes so she could get to the repair work at hand. As she *fwap*-ped up the stairs, her breathing was uncharacteristically heavy, but not because of the physical exertion. The feeling of her first-ever, steamy kiss with Todd was burned into her brain, and no matter what she tried to refocus her mind on, the image kept sneaking back. It wasn't just the kiss. It was also the feelings, the warmth, the pure bliss, and the excitement like a schoolgirl's first kiss. Wendy was processing it all as she ran up the flights of stairs. *Fwap, fwap, fwap.*

What did this mean for their friendship? What did it mean for her Fubar mission? What about that rule she had: no fishing off the company pier? What would she say next time she saw her most loyal friend in the world? Wendy's head started to hurt and she rubbed it, momentarily wondering why there was a lump on her temple. Oh yeah, she thought, remembering how the crabby crappies had all ganged up on her, tossing her headfirst on to the HR lobby floor. She didn't harbor any bad feelings toward them. She knew that their warped *yesterdays* and toxic *todays* were firmly in control of their behavior. It was her job to introduce the crabby crappies to their new *tomorrows*, where bygones could be bygones and forgiveness was unconditional and self-granted.

As she exited the stairwell on the eighth floor, Wendy did something she almost *never* did, she checked her watch. Only one hour until liftoff.

"Shit," she mumbled, and looked around the empty CEO suite, half hoping Todd would pop out of nowhere to reprimand her. But she was alone. Crap! Just a superhero and her Tote of Justice to repair a broken elevator in time to save the world from the crabby crappies of corporate America. Wendywoman sighed and got to work. Trying to push her questions about Todd aside. Trying to stop glancing at her watch. Trying to forget what inevitably waited for her through those CEO suite doors by the end of the day. Trying to forget about the greater enemy who had created him and all like him. Trying to take it one floor and one caustic character at a time. But time was running out on the final arduous day of Wendywoman's mission.

The work was a welcome distraction from all the worrisome thoughts filling her mind. It's hard, and deadly, to be distracted when you're shimmying up and down, over and under an unpredictable elevator carriage suspended precariously eight floors above the ground. Still, she found herself smiling and singing one of Todd's songs, the one he wrote for her after they first met:

> With her Rope of Hope and her mile-high smile
> Once caustic herself who'd have known all the while
> She'd be Wendy… Wendywoman

Then, as she dropped back down into the elevator cab through the roof panel, she remembered the kiss, yet again, and turned a bright shade of red. She eyed the toxicity indicator as she tried to reset it back to green. She couldn't understand why it was still flashing red. "What's the matter with this darn thing?" Then she saw who was entering the elevator and it made sense.

"This stupid thing *never* works," a female voice behind her whined bitterly.

It was Phrantic Phoebe, head of Fubar's Customer Service Department, who hated customers and aimed to provide them with the worst possible service.

"What are *you* doing here?" Wendywoman asked, inadvertently repeating the question that everyone else was constantly asking her. She wasn't trying to be mean; she was just honestly surprised to see the one Fubar employee she had spent the least amount of time with. Yet for some reason, Wendywoman had always thought Phoebe looked familiar. Hmmm, as if they had met before.

"This is where the elevator is," Phoebe said sarcastically in a very "duh" way to Wendy. "Come on, let's go. Snap snap."

Wendywoman looked around the elevator. The lights were back on, motor humming, and even the toxicity indicator was starting to level off. She had no excuses.

"Where do you want to go, Phoebe? Down to the fifth floor?" That was where Customer Service and Phoebe's nest of jaded dissatisfaction with humanity were located.

"No no no!" Phoebe said impatiently.

The hairs on the back of Wendywoman's neck instantly stood straight up, and the sound of fingernails dragging along a chalkboard reverberated throughout her already aching head. She suddenly remembered *exactly* where she had encountered Phrantic Phoebe in her former life.

It was right after the merger of two major American airlines into what would now be known as Divided Airlines. Wendy had been traveling and stepped up to the counter to check her bags and see if she could arrange standby status so she could get home several hours earlier than the original flight she had scheduled.

"Excuse me," said Wendy to the customer service rep. "I'm not really sure how to operate your kiosk. It's not allowing me to fly standby."

"No!" said the "customer service" representative at the airline counter adamantly.

"Well, wait a second. I just would like to get on the standby list," Wendy protested.

"No."

Wendy reminded herself, *Patience: you don't know what's going on in her world.* "Excuse me, but I just want to get my name on the standby list…"

"No."

"You know what? I have platinum status with the other airline, and I'm a little disappointed. I would not expect to get treated like…"

"Oooooh! You have platinum status with [that other airline]?"

Wendy was exasperated. "Yeah."

"Well, you're in the no-no-no line. You're supposed to be in the yes-yes-yes line."

Wendy started laughing. "What?"

"I said, You're in the no-no-no line, and you need to be in the yes-yes-yes line," reiterated the woman.

Instead of just taking care of her right there at the counter, the woman came around front, zeroed Wendy out on that kiosk screen, grabbed her bag, and proceeded to walk her to a different line.

"You got in the no-no-no line, and if you have platinum status you should have gotten in the yes-yes-yes line," explained the woman.

Wendy pinched herself to make sure that she really was in the Denver International Airport and not *The Twilight Zone*. As they walked, she thought, "Oh my gosh, on any given day in the airline industry, how many things are there that they can't control?" Weather, mechanical failures, crabby passengers, and other random flight factors that are uncontrollable. However, the one thing airline employees like Miss No-No-No *can* control in any given moment is how they treat their customers: what they do, what they say, what their demeanor is. They can control that beast. And here this woman was telling Wendy (like a character out of a comic book) that she was in the no-no-no line as she walked her down to the yes-yes-yes line.

When they got to the yes-yes-yes line, the customer service rep said to the new rep, "She was in our no-no-no line. She should have been in your yes-yes-yes line."

Seriously, thought Wendy, looking around the airport terminal, where were the hidden candid cameras? The new rep said, "Oh my gosh, you were in the no-no-no line?" Wendy craned her neck over the crowds, waiting for some young cool celebrity to jump out with his hat on backwards and announce that she had been "kerplunk'd!"

This was clearly a corporate thing at Divided Airlines. It was obviously the way this particular airline viewed its customers. Miss No-No-No, a.k.a. Phoebe, left Wendy with the new rep.

"Oh my gosh, Ms. Komac, what can I do for you?"

"All I'm trying to do is get on a standby list to Cleveland through O'Hare. But if I can't get home by seven, I'll keep what I have."

Click click click went the manicured nails on the keyboard. "There's like twenty-two people in front of you to get on that flight." More clicking. "Okay. You're number one now."

"What's going to happen when I get to Chicago? If I can't make that flight to Cleveland, forget it. I'll bag it and take the direct from here."

Click, click, click.

"Yeah, that one's oversold." Keys again. "Okay. You have a seat there, too." the rep confirmed.

Wendy didn't want somebody else's seat. She wasn't interested in running roughshod over someone else just so she could have the earlier flight. Putting her name on the standby list was something she could control; whether or not she actually got on the flight, well, that was another story altogether. Every day you have things that you control and things you don't control. Knowing the difference is a big deal in how you operate your life.

Obviously, Divided Airlines didn't know the difference. As an organization they had created a culture where that behavior—the no no no—was somehow acceptable and probably even encouraged. It astounded her that a company could be so obviously fubar'd.

Wendy happened to meet Phoebe in that airport. But really, she could have met her anywhere. Phoebe was the unofficial, unauthorized, self-appointed president of the No-No-No Club. All day long she was crabby, crabby, crabby about all the things she couldn't control: weather, flight delays, and mechanical problems. She believed wholeheartedly, but not consciously, in the trickle down effect. The annoyances that came from her superiors, her co workers, and her family—the things she couldn't control—should trickle down to her customers.

It was a mistake to ask her anything; before you got halfway through your sentence, she would likely answer, "No."

> *Don't say another word, just let me guess*
> *I gave you a no when you expected a yes*
> *I wish you would stop wasting my time*
> *Don't tell me your problems or your nightmares*
> *Don't confuse me for someone who cares*
> *If you expected help you're in for a surprise*

Poor Phoebe. If she spent less time worrying about the things she couldn't control and realized that the one thing she did control every day was how she treated her customers, life at the airport would be much more peaceful for everyone, including Phoebe.

Phoebe believed that she needed to have control over things and people in her life to feel good about herself. It was attached and linked inseparably to her self-worth. Her control manifested itself in inappropriate and illogical ways. She tried to control things, even things that either she didn't need to control or that no one really could control. She felt that customers deserved whatever happened to them, and that they should have mitigated their own circumstances. Since they had been forced to come to her for customer service, they were obviously weak. So she justified herself, coming on strong and rationalizing that since they were weak, she deserved to be in control over them and tell them "no." Because "no" is the easiest answer.

"Yes" involved too much work and time on her part. She had to extend herself beyond her comfort level to "help" another person. Of course, she would do it for the "right" person, a platinum person. But in general, when she helped someone else she thought she was putting them in control, and that was not for Phoebe. Phoebe always had to be in control. So, we're back to "no" again.

She rushed to "no." She jumped toward the negative. She dove into big, fluffy piles of "no's," each one delicious to her taste because she craved the power of "no." It was sweet and succulent. There was no threat, no risk, and no fear in her piles. It was her power word that crushed others and made her top dog.

"No" also helped Phoebe control time. She was always in a rush. She hurried through her life of "no" because the faster she moved, the easier it was to say no. Lack of time allowed her to make all her decisions quickly; there was no time for deliberation. She worshipped at the altar of the fast and easy "no."

Weather and mechanical problems will inevitably cause flight delays. Phoebe lived from one disaster to the next simply so that she could tell any unfortunate complainers her spiel of "No!" "Sorry!" "Nothing I can do!"

Saying no was also Phoebe's way of dealing with any sort of failure that might come from making the wrong decision. What she didn't know is that failure doesn't happen overnight, but is a few errors in judgment repeated every day. And failures and losses are all part of success. Like the rest of Fubar's crabby crappies, Phoebe was not a bad person. She was just shortsighted, misinformed, and poorly programmed. Who's got control of our programming? Are we a product of our environment or do we create our environment?

There was no way that Wendy or Phoebe could have known that day in Denver that their paths would cross again here at Fubar, and at that very moment in the elevator currently descending from Floor 8.0.

"So if you don't want to go back to your floor, Phoebe, where do you want to go?" Wendywoman asked, trying to get the hairs on her neck to relax again.

"The employee break room. There's a meeting there that you're not supposed to know about. No, no, no elevator operators allowed," said Phoebe, swimming lazy laps around the confines of her no-no-no comfort zone.

Wendywoman hit the rarely used button that would take them to Floor 5.5, where the employee break room was located. Then, she deployed the Force Field from her MFHD as protection from what might await her there. Wendywoman rarely used the Force Field. Turning it on created an invisible wall between her and the rest of the world, and if she weren't careful, it was easy to misuse. Most people put up invisible walls because they don't want to associate with people. They use an unseen barrier to keep people out that don't look the same, talk the same, walk the same, or believe in the same things. Wendywoman didn't want to live behind a force field. How boring life would be if it were not for diversity. She made a mental note to mention that to Box of Rocks Bill when she saw him, since he loved living life on autopilot—no diversity allowed.

In the meantime, she reminded herself that it was extra important that she use the Force Field only to keep the negativity out, but at the same time to send out love, no matter how impossible that seemed, to all those caustic characters who were so easy to despise. How many times in her life had she done just that? Looked past all the bad qualities someone had only to find a level of greatness within that person that he or she was surprised even existed. She loved when that happened. It was the part of her job that inspired her the most and kept her going when she was up to her ass in alligators. But enough of that for now. Trouble was brewing, and she had to deal with the situation at hand.

Wendywoman stepped back in the elevator, leaned against the railing, and studied little Miss No-No-No. Phoebe stood at the very front of the elevator, poised to tell anyone else who might want to board, "No no no, it's my elevator. You have to take the yes-yes-yes steps."

Not so ironically, Phoebe had once been Miss Yes-Yes-Yes herself. When she first starting working at Divided Airlines, she was a shining example of everything great customer service is supposed to be. She kept three items at the ready beneath her customer service counter in the bustling airport terminal: a laminated copy of the corporate core values, encouraging employees always to say "yes yes yes" to the customer who is "always, always, always" right; a self-help book called *Yes Yes Yes You Can*; and a wire-bound journal that the airline gave to all new customer service employees to record customer comments. The airline encouraged its employees to ask all customers if they were satisfied with the customer service delivered to them; not because they cared, but in accordance with their phony philosophy of "everything you say and do is supposed to make *us* look good." From day one, hour one, and minute one of her career with the airline, Phoebe had cheerfully asked each customer if he or she had been happy with the service and diligently recorded the answers along with the exact date and time.

By the end of Phoebe's first day on the job, her journal was chock-full of customer service experiences (while many of her tenured coworkers had barely gotten to page two). As the company manual had instructed her, Phoebe rushed the journal upstairs to her boss's executive office to share all that she'd learned, which she knew would undoubtedly teach the airline valuable lessons about how to improve as a company. Phoebe felt proud to be a part of such an important process and thought about how lucky she was that Divided Airlines wanted input from its employees.

"No no no," said her boss, flipping impatiently through her pages.

Phoebe's jaw dropped.

"What do you mean?" she asked with a look of a wounded puppy on her face.

"You're being too nice to these suckers," her boss said. "You keep telling them, 'yes yes yes' and listening to what they have to say."

"But I thought…"

"You," said her boss, jabbing his finger in her face, greasy from the abundance of fried food available downstairs in the terminal, "work in the no-no-no line."

"No no no," Phoebe murmured to herself thoughtfully, trying on the words for size.

"Here," he said, handing her back her journal and a permanent marker. "I want you to write this on the front of your journal, 'No No No,' so you don't accidentally forget again."

Still perplexed but wanting to be a good soldier, Phoebe scrawled the phrase in large black letters across the front of her notebook.

Phoebe left her boss's office and returned to her customer service post. From that point on, she took him literally. Sometimes bosses don't understand that when they tell employees to do something, certain employees will take it literally, whether that was the intent or not. It went right in line with Wendy's thinking that bad information delivered the right way is more meaningful than good information delivered the wrong way. Phoebe heard her boss loud and clear. Whenever anyone wanted to know anything, do anything, or get anything, Phoebe would glance down at her journal, look back up at the customer, and say firmly, "No no no." She got rid of the self-help book, replacing it with *The Official Government TSA Guide to Telling Passengers to Stand Still, Shut Up, Spread Their Legs, and Do Everything We Tell Them to Without an Explanation* book.

Back in the elevator, Phoebe looked up at the floor indicator as they were passing Floor 7.0, home of Maniacal Mean Marsha. Wendywoman saw her roll her eyes. Safe within her Force Field, she was feeling brave. Her inquiring mind wanted to know.

"What's with the eye roll?" she asked Phoebe.

Phoebe, like the others, seemed surprised that she wasn't alone in the elevator.

"Don't ask," she said, dismissing the elevator operator.

"But what if I did ask anyway," Wendywoman challenged her. The sun was on its way to setting, and she was sick of messing around.

Phoebe stared at her for so long that Wendywoman thought maybe Serena had shown Phoebe where the "catatonic" switch was in her brain. But then, Phoebe started talking, telling Wendywoman all about the eye roll.

As it turns out, Wendywoman wasn't the only Fubar employee to have encountered Phrantic Phoebe at her airline customer service desk in her prior life. Shortly after Wendywoman's own experience at Divided Airlines, Maniacal Mean Marsha found herself in the middle of Phoebe's no-no-no line. Marsha was in the middle of refusing to let a fellow passenger borrow the pencil she was using to do a crossword puzzle.

"But, ma'am, I just need it to write down the change in my flight plans," the desperate woman, with two whiny brats at her feet, begged Marsha. "I'll be standing right here, so it's not like I'm going to steal it."

Marsha pretended to concentrate on her puzzle, but a satisfied smirk was forming in the corners of her mouth.

"That's not the point," said Marsha.

"Then what is the point?"

"It's my pencil, and you should have brought your own pencil if you thought you might need it. That'll teach you not to be stupid," Marsha fired back.

The woman slunk away, looking as if she might start whining along with her kids.

Then, something else caught Marsha's attention up at the customer service desk.

"No no no," the woman at the desk was saying to an elderly couple.

"But, dear, we need to get home to see our grandchildren," the couple protested.

Marsha was pleased to see that the woman was unmoved. "You can't. Step aside for the next passenger." The elderly couple had no choice but to leave the counter.

By the time Marsha arrived at the counter, after watching her fellow Miss No-No-No rightfully punish several other slackers and losers in front of her, she had a big evil smile pasted across her big evil face.

"What do you want?" Phrantic Phoebe asked quickly, her head down, click-click-clicking away on her keyboard purposefully to delay the next customer.

"I want to know if you're looking for a new job."

Phoebe looked into Marsha's eyes, saw something familiar, smiled, and, for the first time since her first day at Divided Airlines, said "yes."

It was a match made in caustic character heaven. And that's how Phrantic Phoebe left Divided Airlines and came to bless the Fubar Customer Service Department with her cheerful presence.

Wendywoman was just about to ask Phoebe about the eye roll again. What could possibly have gone wrong with her and Marsha's obviously made-to-be friendship? Both women used words as weapons and believed they should control the world around them. But before Wendywoman could ask, they reached their destination, Floor 5.5, the employee break room. The undoubtedly fascinating saga of the wicked witches, thought Wendywoman, would have to wait.

The doors opened, and Phoebe speed walked toward the glass door marked "Break Room." That was the room where the non-executive Fubars went when they needed a break because they were about to crack. Wendywoman was desperately curious to find out why, according to Phoebe, they were desperately cracking all at once. As soon as the door closed behind Phoebe, she locked the elevator and ran over to the door so she could eavesdrop outside the break room.

"Where does she get off anyway? She's *just* an elevator operator after all!"

Wendywoman grimaced, recognizing the voice as Lame-O Leo.

"Yeah!" Box of Rocks Bill agreed. "We don't have to go up to the roof if we don't want to."

"What's going on? Executives in the break room instead of in the Memory Loss Lounge upstairs?" This was bigger than Wendywoman thought.

"Besides she's not even *allowed* up there," agreed Not Me Lee.

"Serena, for goodness' sake, what's with that *stupid* phone again?" Bill yelled.

"Relax, it's not what you think," said Serena, her sappy words trailing off. "I'm letting everybody else know what we're planning so they can help. I created it as a private Facebook event so she can't see."

"Yeah, because *elevator operators* are on Facebook," snorted Marsha, adding, "Loser!" just for good measure to get her point across.

"We're not going to let her get away with this. No no no, we're not," insisted Phoebe.

"The roof. I mean the *roof!* The freakin' *roof!*" Not Me Lee roared angrily.

Listening outside, Wendywoman knew that they'd somehow figured out one of her secrets. As much as she had tried to remain vague about the "sunset ride" and not give any specifics about what a ride to the roof would entail, she knew that somehow word had leaked. And she knew exactly who leaked it—the only person who had everything to lose if the people inside the organization "changed." He had figured out her plan! She also knew, since the scent of rotten eggs wasn't wafting from under the door, that he wasn't in there. Coward! She knew he had specifically leaked this information to them so they would do what he didn't have the balls to: take out his enemy.

Ugh! If there was one thing Wendywoman couldn't stand, it was people, especially those in leadership positions, who couldn't have tough conversations; the ones who always wanted someone else to do their dirty work. Worse yet, they swept all their dirty work under the rug where no one else could see. Or so they thought. It seemed so transparent to everyone but them that the so-called secret sh*t was piling up under the rug. Hell, it was so lumpy under there that the company's liability insurance would undoubtedly double, as someone was bound to trip over the rug and get seriously injured.

"What are *you* doing here?" a man's voice behind her sneered.

She looked up from her crouch. Yet another caustic character had snuck up on her—actually swum up upon her: Sharkman Zak towered over her with his sleazy salesman's smile. He was one of the most dangerous people who could have found her out there. She was lucky those sharp teeth hadn't taken a chunk out of her back when she wasn't looking.

"I was looking for you," Wendywoman said quickly.

"Well, here I am, baby," Zak said, striking a heroic pose.

She knew he didn't buy her fib for a minute, but it wasn't his style to tell people what he thought of them to their faces. He'd save that for one of his backstabbing, backbiting "Zak Attacks," as Wendywoman called them. He much preferred to turn the attention back to himself.

"But," Zak said, pretending to be playful and wagging his finger at her like she was being a naughty little girl. "You know Serena from HR is in there, and if she found out about this, she'd fire you in a minute." He let out an artificial laugh that made Wendywoman's skin crawl. "But don't worry," he winked in an equally creepy way, "I won't tell her."

Even "just an elevator operator" could tell Zak was lying through his big, white, jagged shark teeth.

GATEWAY

ENTER   EIGHT

http://bit.ly/yOHNr4

IN SUMMARY...

So, it took just one bad boss to instantly transform trusting "yes yes yes" Phoebe into controlling "no no no" Phrantic Phoebe. Haven't we all had bosses like that? We start a job with joy and great expectations with the company jargon of ethics, integrity, accountability, and excellent customer service lighting our way. Watch out, world! The employee of the century works here now. Then, the moment we try to shine and spread our wings, the incompetent boss throws water on the flames and clips our wings. It's enough to turn anyone's song from yes-yes-yes to no-no-no, isn't it? In the end, it takes a lot more than some sugary yes-yes-yes motivational messages to change the tune. Here are some strategies.

Phrantic Phoebe's Step: Inviting Discipline into Your Life

❖ Sloppiness in life allows more variables to creep in and spoil your plans.

• Tighten up!

• Identify the things that *you* can control.

❖ Failure is a few errors in judgment repeated every day.

• Failure doesn't happen overnight.

• Don't believe in or settle for failure.

❖ Stop stressing over things you can't control.

• Lighten up!

• Release all things where you have no impact.

❖ Play to win? Sure, but lose like a champion.

• Failures and losses are all part of success.

• Make each loss a useful gain for growth and change.

CHAPTER 8

SHARKMAN ZAK

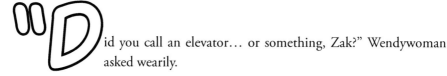id you call an elevator… or something, Zak?" Wendywoman asked wearily.

The lying lips briefly closed over the big shark teeth for a moment as Sharkman Zak thought about her question. Then he gestured towards the closed break room door. "I'm not sure *anyone* around here trusts you and your elevator at this point, lady. Strange things have been happening around the building today, and a lot of people are looking in *your* direction," he lashed out at Wendy.

"Well then, maybe I should go in and clear my name, eh, Zak? I think that would be the right thing to do in this situation. Don't you? Maybe I should tell everyone what you've been telling me out here." Wendywoman managed to keep her calm, challenging Zak to back up his verbal warnings.

"Oh no, I wouldn't do that. They'll eat you alive in there." Zak briefly backed down in the tug of war, suddenly aware of what his colleagues would say if they knew he was talking to her.

"Enough of this," Wendywoman mumbled. Fully prepared to follow through on her promise of busting up the "let's get Wendy" party happening in the break room, she started to open the door, but someone was on the way out at that very moment.

"Todd!" she gasped.

Two faces turned beet red, and the third bared his shark teeth, enjoying their angst.

"And *everyone* knows about *that,* too!" Zak chortled triumphantly.

 Wendy and Todd ignored shark face.

"What are *you* doing in there?" Wendy asked in astonishment.

"Making sure things don't get out of hand," said Todd, eyeing Sharkman Zak with a stern "don't mess with me" look that Wendy had never seen before on his face.

"But why would they even bother plotting against me with you there?" Wendy asked him.

Todd laughed his easygoing laugh, and Wendy was almost sure that recent Fubar events, including that shared kiss between them in the stairwell, were forgotten. "Do you think any of those people even *noticed* the one-armed guy from Marketing sitting quietly in the corner, openly eavesdropping on everything they're planning?" Todd asked.

Wendy knew they hadn't. Up until a few hours ago, they had barely paid attention to her. She noticed that as soon as Todd pointed out his "handicap," Sharkman Zak's cocky demeanor faded. He looked away and was visibly squirming, clearly uncomfortable on a personal level with what he saw as Todd's traumatic childhood past. Zak's natural inclination was to judge people based on first impressions without considering their *yesterdays*. He wasted too many precious moments labeling other people instead of celebrating their individuality. It was his way to shift negative perceptions on everyone else; that way he didn't have to deal with his own glaring issues.

Therefore, once he mentally slapped the label "one-armed Marketing guy and nothing more" on Todd's forehead, Zak's flash of humanity quickly swam back into the deep, and the fraudulent 'Yo friend, how ya doin'?'" returned.

"Hey guys, I just need to go back in and make an appearance, so nobody's suspicious. I'll be right back, and we can take that elevator ride," Zak said, bolting through the door and slamming it behind him before Wendywoman could ask where he needed to go. The Sales and Marketing floor was only half a floor up, and the Sharkman's fins didn't look too broken to use the steps.

"C'mon, let's go," Todd said, grabbing her arm with a concerned look on his face and propelling her toward the elevator.

"What? Why?" Wendywoman asked, confused.

"I have a bad feeling about this. Let's get out of here."

They were only steps away from the elevator when all hell broke loose.

Led by Zak, the mob swarmed from the break room toward Wendywoman and Todd. Anyone else would have interpreted the looks in their eyes as rage. Wendywoman saw it as fear of the unknown—but that didn't stop her from bolting into the elevator as fast as her legs could carry her. She knew that Zak had flipped faces the moment the break room door closed behind him, telling the entire cast of crabby crappies inside that she was outside that door and that she was onto them.

"Get her!" Box of Rocks Bill yelled, egging the other damaged, terrified souls toward the elevator. They obediently followed, as they all considered urgent motion to be the best remedy for fear. Somehow in the mayhem, Zak got shoved into the elevator with Todd and Wendywoman, and the doors closed in front of all three of them. He looked as surprised and terrified as anyone. He looked up at the floor indicator—5.5.

"Where are we…"

Before Zak could finish his sentence, before Wendywoman could confront him about his two-faced treachery, and before Todd could remind himself that he wasn't afraid of elevators anymore—

Whoooshhhh!

Wendywoman didn't even have time to press a floor button before the lights went out and the elevator collapsed under the weight of all the toxicity, the car plummeting to the basement in what all three assumed would be a violent collision. They braced for impact and possibly their respective final exits. Time slowed down as a different movie played in each of their minds.

Physically, Zak was crouched in the back corner of the elevator reaching up and grabbing the railing with white knuckles. Mentally, however, he was exiting his shiny new BMW on a sunshiny day with a big smile on his face in the driveway of the home he shared with his wife and sixteen-year-old son. It was five years ago when he had become Fubar's most successful sales manager in record time. Back then, he was a positive thinker, positively minded, honest, ethical, and everyone in his department wanted to be just like him. This was also around the time that Todd came to work there, and Todd had been impressed by the creative, positive vibe that Zak had created on the Sales and Marketing floor. In fact, Zak had been one of the main reasons that Todd had accepted the marketing job at Fubar.

The *yesterday* that Zak was remembering, crouched on the elevator floor, had started off as one of the best of his life. The Sales and Marketing Departments had been rewarded by the old Fubar CEO for their hard work and innovation, and there was this new guy in Marketing named Todd whose creativity and tremendous outlook on life made Zak eager to get to the office every morning. Arriving home from work, Zak walked through the front door, buoyed by the confidence that his life was just perfect.

"I said *no!*"

His wife's uncharacteristically shrill tone startled Zak as he dropped his briefcase in the foyer and entered the living room where his wife and son were clearly engaged in battle. His son Brad was dressed up in his designer duds, clean-shaven and all polished up. Zak smiled—chip off the old block. His boy was already turning into the ladies' man that Zak had been at his age. At the moment, though, his boy was preparing to fire another verbal round at his mother.

"Whoa, whoa, whoa, you two," Zak said, separating them. "What's going on here?"

His son turned to him. "I have been looking forward to this party for a month now, Dad! You know who is going to be there. She even left a love note in my locker today telling me how she can't wait to hang out with me tonight," Brad said, producing a neatly folded piece of pink stationery from his pocket for his father to examine.

Zak examined the "evidence" that his son had presented. "So what's the problem?" he asked his wife, perhaps too casually.

"The problem is," she seethed, furious that Zak wasn't psychically guessing what the problem was, "the party is at the same boy's house where there is no parental supervision. The cops had to bust up his last party *and* busted some of the kids there for drinking and doing drugs."

"But I told you already, Mom, none of us even knew the kids who got busted, and only people we know are invited this time. Plus, my friend's uncle will be there to supervise. It's totally different this time," Brad pleaded.

"And who is this uncle? How do I know he's not your friend's dealer?" countered Mom.

"C'mon, honey, that's not fair," Zak defended his son. "You don't know these people."

"That's the point! I don't like the sound of this." Zak's wife stood her ground. "I say no."

Son and wife both glared at Zak, demanding with their eyes that he break the tie.

"Well, I say yes," Zak said, making to him what seemed like the easiest decision of his day.

If only it were that easy. Winning over a wife is entirely different from selling your sales team on a great new idea. The battle relocated from the living room into the couple's bedroom, and Brad was ordered to wait downstairs on the couch for the verdict. He did, reading and rereading the piece of pink stationery with a foolish little smile on his handsome young face.

An hour later, the foolish little smile had become a big triumphant smile as Brad walked in the front door of his friend's house. Across town, after dropping off his son at the party, Zak had won the battle and was trying to salvage the war by making a beeline into town for a fancy dinner, fine wine, and roses to win over his wife. At the same moment, Brad was awkwardly approaching his girl at the punch bowl. Far from supervising the kids upstairs, Brad's friend's uncle was downstairs having his own party with his own beverages.

By the time Brad was ready to come home, his parents were fast asleep, exhausted from their respective workdays and the war of the roses. Brad rang and rang for a ride, but Zak had accidentally turned the ringer off on the phone, rather than making it louder as he had intended. Brad was stranded at his friend's house knowing that if he broke curfew, his mom would be even angrier than she was when he left.

"Don't worry, kid, I can drop you off. It's no problem," his friend's uncle said, emerging from the basement.

Brad frowned, remembering everything his parents had taught him about taking a ride from a stranger, especially one who smelled like a keg. But, he reasoned, it was a short ride anyway, and at least his parents wouldn't worry about him. So he took the ride.

Ding dong!

Since Zak's phone was still off, the police officers had to come out to the house unannounced to notify Brad's parents that their son was number one in the exit line and hadn't survived the ride home.

Crouched in the corner of the elevator today, Zak's *yesterday* was coming at him in flashes. His wife's fists beating on his chest… blaming him… hating him for taking her son away from her… Tears of anguish and guilt streaming down his face… looking at the stoic faces of the police officers in the doorway, professional, somber, and, Zak knew, eager to get home and hug their own kids as soon as their awful call of duty was over. Because of his *yesterday*, Zak's today was a bitter, jaded one where anyone and everyone around him made better candidates for blame than the man in the mirror.

My own secret tragedy
The thoughts in my head
Won't forget what I said
As I watched you walk out my front door
Now the way that I gain
Is to put others through pain
But it's my tears that spill on the floor

His wife had left him, of course, but his job at Fubar remained. And with the incoming CEO Methane Man, nobody had even noticed the change in Zak, except Todd, who tried to make it his personal task to "fix" the sales manager.

Todd's mission had obviously failed, but he stayed on anyway, hoping to see glimpses of his old friend again. Have you ever judged someone negatively only later to have that person become a good friend? In Todd's case, the opposite happened, and when his good friend Zak entered his downward spiral, Todd was the only one who stuck by him for as long as he could. Just when he had been about to give up on Zak, a new elevator operator by the name of Wendy showed up at Fubar, and Todd learned of her similar life mission to help people. It gave him hope again, hope that was quickly fading, as even Todd was beginning to wonder if any of these people could be saved.

As the elevator continued its downward plunge, it seemed natural that Todd would be thinking of the time he got stuck in the elevator as a kid, but that was not what was on his mind. He was far more concerned about the woman he was holding and about completing their mission together. Todd looked at Wendy. She had buried her head in his shoulder as they held each other, preparing for the end. He glanced at Zak, who was still crouching in the corner. Even in the dark elevator, Todd could see the tears streaming down Zak's face and knew what he was remembering.

As the months had turned to years, Todd realized there was little chance that his old friend Zak would ever be back, so he had refocused all his energy into helping Wendy. He figured that even if he couldn't save Zak, there were many others that the two of them could save together. And Todd and Wendy had, over the past year, formed the most incredible friendship that either one of them had ever experienced. In the process, Todd's creative soul had reawakened from its slumber, and he was writing more songs and making better music than ever before. For a long time now, he had felt like it was time to move on and follow his heart to music, but he knew Wendy needed him at Fubar—she relied on her "partner in crime"—so he stayed out of love and loyalty to her.

This day though, this final mission to save the company, was the worst of any they had experienced together. He felt Fubar's employees physically sucking away a part of the creative, optimistic soul he knew he would need to continue creating his music. If he got any weaker, Todd knew he wouldn't be able to protect Wendy anymore and would be no good to her. It was time for him to go, and he was absolutely dreading telling the woman he cared about and respected more than anyone in the whole world.

As Todd was pondering his inevitable, heartbreaking conversation there in the dark, plummeting elevator, Wendy was remembering a very dark day from her own *yesterday*—the sudden death of her father. It was the catalyst that pushed her over the line from the high school kid who occasionally drank a beer on the way to school to the full-blown, drifting alcoholic, drinking a bottle of vodka a day.

When she finished high school, she traveled out of the country for several weeks, ending up in Dallas, Texas, on the weekend before the Fourth of July. She was on her own, enjoying the freedom she always experienced during her whirlwind adventures. But that weekend she was suddenly overwhelmed by a feeling that she needed to get home—she *had* to get home. The sensation poured over her like a tidal wave, impossible to ignore.

On the evening of June 30, when she called her dad to tell him that she was coming home, he sounded fine. He sounded like Dad. Seemed okay. She wondered if she was being foolish cutting her trip short. What could possibly have been wrong? What was giving her the sinking feeling in the pit of her stomach? Her Dad thought she was calling because she was out of money, but she told him she felt strongly that she wanted to be at home. He reminded her that she was flying on a free travel pass. It was unlikely she would be able to get home because it was a holiday weekend, but she assured him that she would try to fly standby to Chicago and then to Cleveland.

Wendy left the next morning and after a long day of travel, arrived home in Cleveland at 11:30 p.m. Her Dad picked her up at the gate. The whole way home, he was complaining of an upset stomach. She and her mom both asked him if they should take him to the emergency room, but he said no. Just after midnight, he had a massive heart attack and died. He was forty-eight. As far as Wendy was concerned, she died along with him.

For Wendy, that was the beginning of the end. She still made her own choices, but now she made the wrong ones. Nobody else really knew about that specific impetus, hanging there in the background. Like most of the caustic characters at Fubar, she kept her *yesterday* to herself. Five years later she was a real loser in a very dark place. She assumed that nobody knew about her pain or made the connection between death and drink.

It took almost ten years living in a drunken stupor before she finally made the connection and recognized what was not working. She began to make better choices. She hit the power switch in her life. She had set the bar very low for several years working to maximum mediocrity, but now it was about doing her personal best. She began to pay attention to everything. She clung to what mattered and threw the remainder away.

No one understood the pain she went through before she exorcised this demon from her life. That, incidentally, was why Wendywoman *today* had empathy for the employees of Fubar. Each had his or her own *yesterday*, and she knew she could never fully understand what that person had been through. It was her job to guide them to a better *tomorrow*.

At the time, Wendy was ignorant to these revelations. So ten years of her life went by with little progress after she sobered up. Her dad had been gone for almost twenty years, but she was still carrying around guilt about what she might have done differently that night. No one else knew how she was allowing that to impact her behavior. For most people, the only thing they know about another person is the behavior they perceive. That makes their understanding incomplete.

Wendy's first glimpse of using her intuition was her to choice to go home. Not knowing why she should leave Dallas, but that she needed to. What would have happened to Wendy today, where would she be had she not paid attention to her intuition? If she had not seen her father before he died? If she had chosen to blow it all off and keep on her partying ways? All logic said "you can't get home!" but she followed that little voice which made all the difference in the world.

Today's Wendy looked at Todd as they plummeted toward the basement in the dark elevator. Her intuition now suddenly told her it wasn't over. Despite all the toxicity and floor indicators above, they were not first in the exit line as Zak's son had been. It's not over yet, thought Wendywoman with a renewed ferocity. Time to fight!

Hi-yahhhh!

With a burst of physical strength that she never could explain, Wendywoman leapt into the air and kicked the top panel of the elevator out with her red superhero boots, which she didn't even remember putting on. As Zak stopped sobbing long enough to look up, Todd instinctively reached into the Tote of Justice and tossed Wendywoman her Golden Rope of Hope. Saying a silent prayer to her guardian angels, Wendywoman formed a lasso with the rope and, with all her strength, threw it high into the air, praying that something would catch it.

She was promptly thrown back into the elevator. The three occupants were tossed around like rag dolls, landing in a pile on the floor as the elevator screeched to a stop and the doors miraculously opened. Wendywoman looked down; they were just inches from the concrete bottom of the elevator shaft. The experience reminded her that time is the great equalizer, and you must make time for what you love. Will you live before you die? Only if you make your life the priority and have the courage to use *your* voice to send your desires into the world.

She uttered another silent prayer to her guardian angels, before exiting the elevator with the others. Zak quickly wiped his tear-stained face and worked hard to put his shark face back on. Todd looked at him sadly.

That was as close to disaster as Wendy and Todd had ever come together, although there were certainly a lot of natural disasters happening in the world: earthquakes, floods, hurricanes, tsunamis, and wild fires. There was always something bad happening somewhere and Wendywoman watched with wonder as people responded a variety of ways: some willing to help in any way, shape, or form, and others claiming that there was nothing they could do to help. She wished she could remind everyone that during any disaster, there was always something to do. Sure, it might be true that they did not have the money to donate and they didn't own a Golden Rope of Hope as she did, but there was no reason that they could not offer a smile, prayer, or compassion to those in need. Those things were free. And there was absolutely no excuse for not giving them. It was something Zak needed right now.

Zak also needed to understand the concept of forgiveness, one of the most misunderstood words in the English language, in Wendywoman's opinion. All too often we think that forgiveness is for someone who hurt us, and that it somehow lets that person off the hook. But forgiveness, in its purest form, would have been for Zak, so that he could ultimately move on with his life (not to be confused with *forgetting* that the incident ever happened). Then there was the issue of Zak needing to forgive himself for letting his son go to the party that fateful night. Living with the guilt of the accident was eating him alive, and as real as his pain was every day, he was going to make sure everyone suffered along with him. It ruined his marriage, his job, all of his relationships.

"Zak, is there still a chance for any of them?" Wendywoman asked softly, making eye contact with him.

"I… um… you…" Zak stammered, still emotionally straddling his *yesterday* and his *today*. But the battle quickly became too much for him, and Sharkman Zak bolted up the stairwell to join the others in plotting against the woman who had just saved his life.

Wendy faced Todd. "Okay, partner, a couple more stops and then it's the moment of truth." She tried to sound normal, but avoided eye contact nevertheless.

"Wendy, we have to talk," Todd said.

"Can't it wait? I just got my second wind, and it's go time, baby! We can *do* this!" Wendywoman pulled out her elevator repair tools.

Todd looked at her with sadness in his eyes. This wasn't the right time. Would it ever be? He started toward the stairwell. "I'm here if you need me, Wendy," Todd said, opening the door to the steps.

"Thanks, Todd. See you soon!" Wendy waved energetically, already busy with her repairs. She was so engrossed in her mission that she didn't notice that Todd remained in the stairwell, gazing at her through the little glass window, for a few more lingering moments.

http://bit.ly/y10cXL

IN SUMMARY...

Rather than finding the courage to face his own trauma and take responsibility for the choices he made on that fateful night of his *yesterday*, Zak has shaped his *today* around exerting his power over others. He uses the blame game to deflect any arrows of accountability from accidentally piercing his thick skin, and when things get dicey, he switches faces and sinks his shark teeth into his enemy's back as that person walks away, thinking he or she has made a friend.

As we learned, Wendywoman faced her own trauma as part of her *yesterday*. It took her a while, but she managed to find the lesson buried deep in the pain of losing her father and changed her choices in life because of it.

Choice is a powerful word, yet one that many people turn a blind eye to, finding it easier to swim with the sharks. Upstairs at Fubar, that's exactly what Wendywoman's coworkers were doing—preparing for feeding time, rather than figuring out if they were even hungry. Unfortunately, it is Wendywoman who is on the menu.

Sharkman Zak's Step: Life in the Exit Line

❖ Time is the great equalizer.

• Make time for what you love.

• Don't take things personally.

❖ Will you live before you die?

• Make *your* life the priority; everything else is secondary.

• Have the courage to use *your* voice to send your desires into the world.

❖ Our natural inclination is to judge people.

- Don't waste precious moments spending your time labeling anyone: stylish, sloppy, pretty, too thin, too fat, too old, too busy.

- Celebrate your individuality. Be comfortable in your own skin.

- Have you ever judged someone negatively, only to later have that person become a good friend? If so, you have personally experienced the perils of the judgment cycle.

❖ Learn how to dismiss your natural tendency to believe your first impressions.

- It is a complete waste of time—the one thing you can't get an accurate *read* on.

- Try and understand that everyone has a *yesterday*.

❖ Liking or disliking someone is a choice.

CHAPTER 9

MANIACAL MEAN MARSHA

Floor 5.0, 5.18, 5.28… Wendywoman stood in the center of the elevator, hands on her hips like a superhero preparing for battle, as the car rose: 5.35, 5.41, 5.45… She was headed back to the war room, formerly the break room, to retrieve her second-to-last caustic character of the day, and one of the worst. She assumed that Maniacal Mean Marsha was still rallying the troops on Floor 5.5 and wasn't exactly sure how she would extricate the large and in-charge office manager from her minions. But, she thought, squaring her shoulders, a mission is a mission; Marsha must be taken down a few floors from the spires of her power trip—somehow.

Wendywoman checked the readings on all the items in her Tote of Justice. Her Golden Rope of Hope was coiled neatly in the outer pouch. The Immoral Compass, which doubled as her belt buckle, was spinning out of control, especially as the elevator neared Floor 5.5. The elevator call signal on her multifunction hazard detector (MFHD) went off, alerting her that someone in the building needed an elevator ride immediately, and it was coming from floor 5.5! She had a sudden mental image of every last Fubar employee waiting outside the elevator bearing flaming torches and pitchforks.

Wendywoman stepped to one side of the car, in front of the elevator buttons, with her MFHD at the ready as the doors slid open. Phew! No torches or pitchforks in sight. But meoooow! There was a catfight in progress!

"Someone called for an elev—" Wendywoman started to ask as she stepped out of the elevator, when Zak interrupted her.

"I did!" he shouted, trying to wedge himself between the warring parties, Phoebe and Marsha.

Bam! Zap! Pow! Both women used words as their primary weapons of choice while also swiping at each other like cats with extended claws. Wendywoman briefly wondered why Zak was the only male in the hallway watching the stereotypical cat fight, and daring to even try and break it up. She mentally scolded herself for even contemplating such a degrading cliché. She silently awarded Zak extra humanitarian points for his efforts. Then, just as quickly…

"They're interrupting our meeting and just plain getting in the way of things," he explained, pushing the two warring women into the elevator.

"What makes you think *I* can stop them?" Wendywoman asked.

"Oh please, lady! We've all figured out that whenever weird stuff happens around here, you're behind it. Why don't you try another elevator death drop to the basement like you did earlier?" Zak spouted angrily.

Biting her tongue to avoid saying what she was really thinking—namely, that if Zak used that kind of imagination in his sales job, Fubar wouldn't be in such a fubar mess—Wendywoman changed the conversation's course.

"Why don't you join us gals for a ride, Zak? You guys have to be just about done in there." She gestured toward the still-closed break room door.

"Not even close," Zak chuckled. "Besides, I've had just about enough of elevators today." He observed the cat fight for a moment. Phoebe and Marsha didn't appear to have noticed the change in scenery and were viciously battling it out in the back of the elevator. Wendywoman remained outside the elevator, giving the women all the room they needed.

"Yes, you have had a big day, haven't you, Zak?" Wendywoman asked, watching him.

A shadow of vulnerability flickered across Zak's eyes for just a moment, and Wendywoman saw hope. Then the shark swam back, and the eyes turned cold and black again. Zak quickly turned and swam back to the break room, slamming the door behind him. Wendywoman smiled—this was progress, whether he thought so or not.

When she tried to step back into her elevator, two meaty female hands pushed her back out. Marsha filled the elevator doorway, glaring at Wendywoman and daring her to reclaim the elevator. Wendywoman sensed that Marsha's mutiny had officially begun. From behind her, slender Phoebe piped up over Marsha's linebacker shoulder.

"No no no, we need her to push the buttons," Phoebe whined disagreeably.

"Dimwit! I can press a button!" Marsha snorted and stepped over to the elevator panel.

With that, both women started wildly punching buttons, each reaching over the other, throwing elbows and swatting hands in a vain attempt to get the stubborn elevator to move. But nothing happened (although the toxicity indicator rose from green to red above them).

"See? I told you we need her," Phoebe told Marsha triumphantly.

"Where are you ladies going?" Wendy asked diplomatically.

"None of your *bleeping* business," Marsha responded.

The Fubar office manager was glowing with electricity. There were practically sparks flying off her. Wendywoman reminded herself that everybody is made of the same stuff and that it's what you do with your stuff that matters. "Stuff" is like electricity: it can light up a room or electrocute someone. Marsha was maxed out on every connection and firing on all cylinders.

"Isn't the meeting still going on?" Wendywoman asked, hoping to coax them out of her elevator.

"Our part of the meeting is over. The plans are in motion," Marsha said, looking at Wendywoman with lightening daggers in her eyes.

"Where are you going, then?" Wendywoman asked again, resigning herself to the fact that there would be another elevator ride today before sunset.

Ding ding ding! Her question was enough to launch *The Cat Fight of Floor 5.5 Part II*. As the words and claws flew in the elevator, Wendywoman waited patiently outside, reflecting on how these two women who had been destined to be the best of friends instead became fierce enemies.

When Marsha liberated Phoebe—actually Phoebe's customers—from Divided Airlines, the customers remaining in line had let out a whooping, hollering cheer in farewell to Miss No-No-No (little realizing that Phoebe's replacement was Miss "No way, never, are you kidding me, why bother even asking?"). Not that this had been any of Phoebe's concern: she was on her way to the greener pastures (well, browner, actually) of Fubar Corp. As the two walked out of Denver International Airport, Marsha very uncharacteristically had worn a big smile on her big face. The newly anointed office manager had been drowning in a sea of disagreeable Fubar morons who clearly didn't understand that the person who controlled the office pencil supply controlled the world. And after observing Phoebe's no-no-no attitude toward similar morons at the airport, Maniacal Mean Marsha decided that the young woman would make an ideal lieutenant, which is why she had recruited her on the spot.

Little did she know that Phoebe's perspective was a little different. There was a rumor floating around that Divided Airlines was about to divide again and merge with yet another airline. And it was rumored that the people who ran the new airline preferred "yes yes yes" to "no no no." Phoebe wasn't ready for change that drastic. So when the big mean looking woman at her counter asked her if she wanted a golden parachute out, Phoebe grabbed it without a second thought. It was not because she was interested in getting to know this Marsha person better, and certainly not because she shared Marsha's visions of a power partnership to set Fubar straight, she just wanted to make sure her freedom to say "no" was not taken away from her.

This had come as a huge surprise to Maniacal Mean Marsha on Phoebe's first day on the job. Marsha had just exited the elevator, which was operated by the infuriating nobody operator, when she heard Phoebe repeating into a phone the same wonderful words she'd first heard at the airline counter: "No no no!" Marsha settled into an oversized chair in front of Phoebe's desk and enjoyed the show. After a few minutes of "no no no," the unfortunate Fubar customer on the other end of Phoebe's phone line must have realized that he or she was SOL and hung up.

"So how are you enjoying your first day?" Marsha asked.

Phoebe looked surprised to see someone in her office. After the chaos of working at the airport (so many people to say "no no no" to and so little time in one shift), she was hoping to be left alone in her new post. She flipped the switch on her headset to off. "Um… nobody's bothering me…

too much," Phoebe mumbled, staring at the phone, trying to summon another call that would give her something to do. Something other than talk to Marsha, that is.

"Well, it's time to go to lunch. Come on, I'll show you the break room," Marsha said (well, actually ordered), extracting herself from the chair and heading toward the door, assuming her new lieutenant would obediently follow.

"No no no," said Phoebe, using the same tone as always.

Marsha turned slowly, looking like King Kong about to squash New York. "What did you just say?"

The murderous icy daggers Marsha sent Phoebe were enough to stun most people into submission. But Phoebe was barely paying attention now, busying herself with a million other pointless tasks at her desk in hopes of making this annoyance leave her office.

"No no no," Phoebe repeated. "I brought my lunch, and I plan to eat it here."

"Listen, new girl, I don't know if you know who you're saying 'no no no' to. Around here, I'm the person people go to when they need something— office supplies, information, everything! So if you know what's good for you, you'll come to lunch with me so I can give you the lay of the land!" Maniacal Mean Marsha said, attempting to control her rage in hopes of still converting her new recruit.

Most people rarely give thought to how their words or deeds impact others. They never ask themselves, "Do those who walk away from a conversation with me feel appreciated, inspired, or respected? Do they feel liked?" Those who encountered Marsha generally felt the exact opposite: disrespected, flattened, or disliked. It was destructive criticism at its best. Phoebe, however, felt indifferent.

"I said no no no." Phoebe held her ground, staring directly at Marsha with the same dead stare she had used at the airport to make people go away.

"*You* are going to be *sorry*! See what happens next time you need so much as a *pencil*!" Marsha raged. She stormed out of Customer Service.

Phoebe returned to her busywork without as much as a blink of the eye. Despite the fact that she was a newbie there, she had already become yet another one of the walking dead haunting the halls and offices of Fubar.

Here in the present, still waiting outside the elevator, Wendywoman reflected on the slap in the face that Marsha had received from Phoebe that day. It wasn't really Phoebe's fault. She was just being Phrantic Phoebe, just as Maniacal Mean Marsha was being herself. The lesson, Wendywoman mused, was that when two wrong assumptions collide and blood spills, it is up to both disputing parties to backtrack and figure out where the tracks had switched that caused the trains to collide in the first place. Unfortunately for these two, still battling it out in the elevator, ever since that first day they had merely continued to push the trains forward into each other, driving metal into metal until they'd created an unrecognizable wreck of twisted steel.

"Fine, let's go up to your office. I just remembered that I need something anyway," said Phoebe.

Wendywoman almost fell over from shock. That was the closest version of "yes" that she had ever heard Phoebe utter. Marsha smiled triumphantly, and Wendywoman could have sworn she heard the faint sound of steel untwisting a little.

"What do you need?" Marsha asked Phoebe.

"A pencil."

Wendywoman buried her face in her hands as Marsha crowed like a victorious rooster.

"Well, well, well! Then *you* will need to come up to my office and complete the standard—no actually, the *extended*—five-page requisition form to order office supplies. You will need to explain why you need this pencil while also trotting your skinny butt back to Customer Service, so I can perform a thorough inspection of your work area to make absolutely sure that there is not even as much as a pencil *stub* anywhere to be found!"

"No no no no no no!"

That was when Phrantic Phoebe became unglued, losing the power of all speech except her favorite words. Slapping her hands over her ears, she flew out of the elevator and into the stairwell, running back down to the sanctuary of her customer service desk.

Well, thought Wendywoman, at least she took the steps.

She looked at Maniacal Mean Marsha, who was still standing in the middle of the elevator, still hoping the buttons would work for her, still hoping she could control her transportation back to her office. The elevator, of course, remained motionless, with the lights on the floor buttons off.

"What are *you* looking at," Marsha sneered at Wendywoman, folding her arms and staring at the ceiling with her upturned pig nose.

I'm Maniacal Mean Marsha and I'm here to say
if you don't want my opinion you'll get it anyway
I don't know your name... I don't know what you do
but I know for sure that I'm better than you

"Do you still need a ride up to your office, Marsha?" Wendywoman asked.

Marsha said nothing, but stepped aside, allowing Wendywoman back in to operate her elevator again. "Thank you," Wendywoman said cordially, sending the elevator to Floor 7.0. "I see you and Phoebe are getting along better these days," she said, referring to Phoebe's near-yes experience a minute ago.

"Why are you talking to me, monkey girl?" Marsha hissed.

"Monkey?"

"That getup," Marsha said, gesturing at Wendywoman's elevator uniform. "Shouldn't you have an accordion or something?"

Wendywoman didn't need her Force Field up to let Marsha's daggers bounce right off. She had learned a long time ago that daggers coming from an attacker's *yesterday* have about as much power to destroy you as a foam dart. It had taken her a while to learn that lesson, but it had finally sunk in. So, while the toxicity indicator continued its steady climb toward red, she changed the subject to a much more important one. Knowing that she probably only had one shot at this, Wendywoman chose her words carefully.

"Marsha, what is it about today that made everyone so angry with me, more so than any other day?"

Marsha looked up in surprise. She clearly wasn't expecting that and was momentarily, and historically, speechless for a moment. Wendywoman saw that as an invitation to continue. "I would love to know what I did or said specifically today that set off whatever it is that you're all planning down there. I know you're not at liberty to tell me what you're planning, but is there any reason you can't at least tell me what set everyone off?"

Marsha's surprise quickly transformed back to the familiar icy daggers. Wendywoman listened calmly, careful to keep a neutral expression on her face, so that Marsha would share the truth rather than reacting to what she saw as situational hostility.

"You know what you did, monkey woman? What you *always* do! You keep trying to *change* people! We know. We got together and compared notes about what you do, what you've done—whatever it is you're doing—to all of us. And we don't like it! So we've been trying to figure out a way to stop you. Who put you in charge anyway?" The elevator arrived on Floor 7.0, Marsha's office. "So now you know!" Marsha said, as if that were the end of it, and then tottered down the hall to her office in her two-inch heels.

Wendywoman quickly locked the elevator and took off after Marsha, with her Tote of Justice in tow. "And you don't see any reason to change what you don't see as broken, right, Marsha?" Wendywoman asked, trying to find agreement with Marsha.

"Go back to your elevator, lady. What's done is done," Marsha said as she unlocked the door to her office and entered. Wendywoman followed close behind. "Oh no, you don't!" she yelled as she tried to push the door shut on Wendywoman.

"Give me a break, Marsha," said Wendywoman, pushing back with all her strength. "Why are you all so afraid of the roof?"

Marsha stopped pushing as Wendywoman fell into her office. Sniff, sniff… This office always seemed to be permeated by a lingering smell of bleach. Marsha rushed behind her desk to shield herself from any sudden attacks of "change."

The smell of bleach reminded Wendywoman of how it was that Fubar had come to be blessed with Maniacal Mean Marsha's presence in the first place. Several years earlier, Marsha had been the head of Fubar's overnight cleaning crew. What was now the Office Manager's office on the seventh floor, had once been the Fubar cleaning closet. One night, Marsha was polishing the furniture upstairs in the Executive Suite. Even though she'd only been there a few weeks, she sensed something was different about the suite. There always seemed to be at least a few executives hanging out there, even late at night. It was as if their memories were wiped clean, and they'd forgotten to go home. As she wiped away the food stains and coffee cup circles from the expensive furniture, she was suddenly overcome by the smell of rotten eggs. She looked up to find the company's new CEO looking at her with a confused expression on his face.

"Where can I find some office supplies? I can't find anyone to help me," said Methane Man.

Rather than explain to him that the reason he couldn't find anyone was because it was three o'clock in the morning, Marsha decided to help him herself, using one of the keys from her master ring. From that point on, word spread throughout the Memory Loss Lounge that when in doubt, about anything, office supply related or otherwise, Marsha was the one to ask. If you didn't know what to do, she would tell you. If you needed something, she would get it for you.

Marsha was immediately buoyed by her newfound power. She would be the new power strip locator and label maker of everyone at Fubar. She was now a Very Important Person. Accordingly, she decided that such an important cog in the gears of corporate America needed an office. Since she was never officially hired and nobody *really* knew she was there, Marsha converted her cleaning closet into an office, slapped a placard engraved with "Office Manager" (courtesy of one of those mall kiosks) on the door, and switched from the night shift to the day shift.

Now, she sat there, squeezed behind her desk, glaring at Wendywoman suspiciously.

"What do you think is going to happen on the roof?" Wendywoman pressed.

"You're going to get us all fired, that's what!" Marsha said, tacking an expletive onto the end of her remark for good measure.

"Is *that* what you think?" Wendywoman asked, while secretly knowing that Marsha and the other crabby crappies weren't far from the truth. But ultimately, that was going to be their choice.

"Did you need something? A pencil, perhaps? Although I don't know what an elevator operator would do with a pencil. Do you people even know how to write?" Marsha once again returned to her toxic comfort zone. And once again, the toxic daggers bounced right off Wendy. Nevertheless, with her hands shielded from view by the desk, Wendywoman reached into the Tote of Justice and started powering up everything in it. She knew that since Marsha was the ringleader—most of the executives feared her wrath—getting through to her and convincing her to give the sunset elevator ride a shot would give Wendywoman a chance to get the others on board—literally.

Whrrrr! Zzzt! Wendywoman powered up the MFHD, preparing to scoop any poop that Marsha dumped in her lap, detect and destroy any BS attacks, and trap any Venus Lies that came her way. The only thing she didn't power up was her Force Field. In this situation, she would need to stay as emotionally connected as possible. She slid out the Golden Rope of Hope.

"Oops!" Wendywoman knocked over a container of pencils and stooped down to pick them up. Marsha rolled her eyes, but by this point, she had deployed her own toxic Force Field around herself and had almost forgotten Wendywoman's presence. Down on the floor on her hands and knees, Wendywoman looped the Golden Rope of Hope in a circle around Marsha's feet. Then she scooped up the pencils and climbed back into the chair. Already, the transformation was remarkable.

Marsha was staring straight across the desk at Wendy, but her mind was elsewhere. It was as if she had just been shot by an elephant tranquilizer gun full of truth serum. She was ready to talk. But Marsha didn't talk about the roof or Fubar or what her co-workers were plotting. Instead, she started a strange series of reenactments of a little girl in parochial school decades before. Wendywoman wondered for a moment if the Fubar office manager had been possessed by the devil. Marsha's entire demeanor had changed from vicious office power monger to vulnerable little girl with a child's voice to match. Wendywoman's tools had done the job, stripping away every last layer of Marsha's BS, and all that was left was her childhood. Marsha started to reenact a scene straight out of elementary school, alternating her little girl's voice with an older, harsher voice, presumably that of a nun. Wendywoman couldn't help but notice the similarity between the nun's voice and adult Marsha's voice. They could have been mother and daughter.

"I need a new pencil," Marsha said, sounding like a seven-year-old girl. Marsha then imitated the sound of a ruler going WHAP followed by a little girl's whimper.

"Young lady, you *have* a pencil already!" said Marsha in the strict, icy voice of a parochial school nun.

"But it's too small for me to write with," said little Marsha.

There was another *whap* to her knuckles and another whimper.

"Young lady, you will use every *last* inch of that pencil until there is nothing left but the eraser," hissed the nun's voice.

"But—it's—just—a—pencil," little Marsha was now sobbing, confused at why a pencil was being made to upset her so much.

Whap! Whimper.

"It's a sin to waste that pencil. You will use every last inch of it."

"But… too small to hold," sobbed little Marsha.

"That's *it*, young lady! You're a bad girl! A very bad girl! It's down to the boiler room for you to be paddled!"

Back in present time, in the office manager's office that smelled faintly of bleach, Maniacal Mean Marsha frowned with a tearful look on her face, rubbing her hand, as if the wounds from the nun's ruler were still fresh, still hearing the voice in her head when the nun told her she was a bad, bad girl. Words can be dangerous weapons; once spoken, you can't take them back. Physical wounds can often heal quickly, but emotional wounds linger, sometimes remaining raw forever.

Wendy could see the piercing pain caused by the labels the nun had applied to Marsha. Wendy called them labels and lies—destructive criticism—and she had had her fair share stuck to her, though she had ripped many of them off. How many times in her life had people told her what she wouldn't be, couldn't be, and what they thought she should be and was? How many times had she downright ignored them? Pretty much always. Wendy smiled when she thought of how she had taught her own kids, Lexi and Cory, to ignore the labels others tried to put on them and how it often got them in trouble in school. Oh well, at least they would grow up independent, deciding their own master plans for life, not leaving their fates to the hands of others. Wendy could spend a whole day dealing with that issue alone, but she couldn't take the time. The clock was ticking. It would be sunset soon.

Wendywoman had not had particularly high hopes for Marsha's redemption, so was thinking she would have to give in and power down her tools. Then Marsha looked up with a tearful expression, much to Wendywoman's surprise. She looked almost… apologetic.

Wendywoman decided to press on. "Why can't you just take a chance on creating a new *tomorrow* for yourself, Marsha? What's the worst that could happen?"

Marsha continued to rub her hand. "It's not up to me," Marsha said. "If I was really in charge, don't you think I'd still be downstairs with the rest of them in the break room?"

"If it's not up to you, then whom?" Wendywoman asked.

"*Him*," Marsha said, rolling her eyes upward and recalling her first encounter with the CEO in the Memory Loss Lounge as she polished the furniture while working on the cleaning crew. "He's just sticking the blame on me for his power trip. He's planning something worse, though," said Marsha. "Not just for you, but for all of us, too. For everyone except *his kind*."

GATEWAY

ENTER

TEN

http://bit.ly/zdHRWP

In Summary...

Wendywoman is getting closer and closer to the sunset ride to the top of the building. And now, finally, Marsha has given Wendywoman the information she needs to stop the caustic plan to thwart her mission. Marsha! Of all people: the cleaning lady turned accidental office manager. At least now we know how Fubar's biggest control freak grew such a thick skin to block out the world from her view atop her power pedestal. A pencil, a nun, some mean-spirited words, and the repeated whack of a ruler in Marsha's *yesterday* contributed to who she was *today*. And ever since, Marsha has doled out her own ruler smacks to anyone who dared cross her, using her words. Have you ever come across a Maniacal Mean Marsha in your office? You probably have; we all have. How did you deal with her?

Maniacal Mean Marsha's Step: Power versus Force

❖ Everybody is made of the same stuff; it is what you do with your stuff that matters.

  • "Stuff" is like electricity: it can light up a room or electrocute someone.

  • Most people rarely give thought to how their words or deeds impact others.

❖ Stop and ask yourself: Do those who walk away after meeting me feel appreciated, inspired, respected? Do they feel liked?

  • Remember: You may think you are a good person deep down, but it is your external landscape, not your blissful inner landscape, that most people can see.

❖ Words can be dangerous weapons because you can't take them back.

- Physical wounds can often heal quickly, but emotional wounds linger and sometimes never heal.

- There are no degrees of honesty, only absolutes. Either you are honest or you are not. If you cannot be truthful in what you say and be loving in how you say it, don't say anything at all.

❖ Delivery is worth more than the words you speak. Bad information delivered the right way will get you farther than good information delivered the wrong way.

- Are you someone who lights up the room or darkens the doorway?

CHAPTER 10

METHANE MAN

CHAPTER 10: METHANE MAN 175

THE FINAL BATTLE...

on of a *bleep*!"

Wendywoman was more furious than she'd ever been in her entire life. This time he had gone *too* far. She knew he was the most caustic character and the root of all evil at Fubar, but she had never expected this. Ever. "Benefits cut... layoffs... outsourcing... triple work for those left behind... except for the executives... the executives..."

Maniacal Mean Marsha's words played over and over in Wendywoman's head as she ran breathlessly up the stairs toward the CEO suite, seething more with every step. The toxic golden parachute that Methane Man had swooped in on was about to suffocate most of the company. Considering where he had come from, however, Wendywoman knew she shouldn't be surprised at any level of evil that Methane Man was capable of. He was, after all, perhaps the most toxic of all by-products created by the worst caustic character ever, the source of all evil in corporate America and beyond: Methane Mom. Methane Mom had methodically circulated through the sewer systems of corporate America.

Bet you didn't know that benevolent Mother Earth has an evil counterpart. As much as Mother Earth represents everything that is good, Methane Mom represents everything that is evil. She spawns all the crabby crappies, including the ones who Wendywoman regularly dealt with at Fubar, and the ones the rest of us deal with every day. She is the source of all the toxic *yesterdays* that constantly create polluted *todays*. To most of us, she can seem unstoppable, since just when a cleanup of corrupt executives is complete, another corporate gang is revealed. It can seem that Methane Mom's ability to produce the toxic sludge masquerading as leaders, infiltrating what used to be some of the most prestigious corporations in the world, is endless.

A case in point: Methane Man had managed to finagle his way into Fubar Corp., and now, it was time for him to go. He really was a piece of work. From a young, impressionable age, Methane Man had quickly learned to grab onto any corporate coattails he could get his little toxic fingers around. Once he grabbed hold, he never let go, coasting on his golden parachute from one job to the next, spewing his crap all over corporate America and causing moral and economical bankruptcy from sea to shining sea.

Gee, does this remind you of any modern day Methane Man characters? So many of our leaders are charter members of the Wretchedly Unhappy Club. Are you a member—or your friends, or family, or colleagues? If so, do you recall being initiated, or did you somehow just find yourself at a club meeting one day and wonder how you got there? The good news is that the door works in both directions. You can leave. How? Refine your inner circle. Remember that you become the company you keep. And if that company includes the likes of Methane Man… run! Run fast, run screaming, and don't look back.

All grown up, more toxic than ever, and thanks to a little string pulled by Methane Mom (she tended to do this for her most promising caustic children), Methane Man soon found himself at the helm of one of the world's largest global investment banks: Lair Sterns. He landed the gig despite never actually having learned anything about global investment or even math, for that matter. In fact, he'd been floating along on someone's coattails since his very first math class as a kid when he started copying off Billy Reynolds, who learned the hard way to be properly terrified of Methane Boy. After threatening to tell on Methane Boy, Billy found a pile of poop where his bike was supposed to be after school one day. Well, if you put two and two together (as Methane Man obviously could not), you'd quickly foresee the fate of Lair Sterns: a major contributor to the worst bankrupting of the global market the world had ever seen.

As Wall Street crumbled, Methane Mom observed the chaos from a rooftop nearby, wearing a big evil smile on her face. She spent almost all her time on corporate rooftops, hatching her next evil plan and yanking on all her little soldiers' toxic puppet strings, telling them each what to do, where to go, and when to do what. In Methane Man's case, as the assets of Lair Sterns spiraled down the drain, Methane Mom also told him it was time to unpack his golden parachute and float to his next opportunity for mayhem.

Methane Mom scanned the corporate rooftops of New York City with a contented sigh. Her work there was done for the time being. The financial heart of corporate America, and the rest of the world for that matter, had been significantly blackened by Methane Man and his loyal lieutenants, including a promising new intern named Not Me Lee. It was time to move on.

But where would she go next? Her Evilness had considered another large market like Los Angeles, but the sins of Hollywood that she had embedded years ago were still actively spreading their toxic gases. On a particularly smoggy day in L.A., if you look up, you can sometimes see the outline of Methane Mom's face, smiling down from the static sediment hanging over the city, admiring her good work.

No, it was time for her precious boy Methane Man to hit a smaller market and lay low, somewhere he could bide his time while he infused corporate America with his lying, cheating toxic gases. Methane Mom looked west across the rooftops of the big Apple to the Midwest and… Cleveland, Ohio. Perfect! Who could there possibly be in Cleveland, who could stop her and her son, or even dare to try? No one. Or so Methane Mom thought.

Later that month, there was a secret midnight meeting held by the board of directors of a corporation in Cleveland. This was a few years before a certain elevator operator had joined the company and even before a certain large and in-charge cleaning lady had started polishing the executive wood in the Memory Loss Lounge. The meeting had taken place in the corporate conference room, which was later absorbed into the Sales and Marketing Departments. Back then, the board simply didn't see the need for such a waste of money since funds were funneled into the company without any actual customer transactions.

The board members weren't at all bothered by the stench of methane that heralded Methane Man's arrival into the conference room. With the lights turned off and only the light of the moon shining in the windows, they motioned for the former Lair Sterns CEO to take a seat at the head of the table. The stealth meeting was simply a formality. The board had already done its "due diligence" and knew exactly what Methane Man was all about: by then it was all over the news and the topic of conversations around the world. The average person was in disbelief at how at how this alien race of "Wall Street fat cat" clones were able to commit such awful acts of treason on the American people without compunction. The media, "on behalf of" the people, were calling for Methane Man's head on the proverbial platter.

The Fubar board of directors, however, had decided tales of his malfeasance and incompetence had been a giant misunderstanding, and they were pleased to welcome the smiling, charming man, in his gray silk suit, and his hair slicked back, currently sitting at the head of their conference table and promising them the world. The world's most notorious financial criminal smiled, charmed, and dazzled his fellow kings of the corporate universe, walking their walk and talking their talk just as Methane Mom had trained him and all her other caustic creations to do. He was one of them, and by the end of the meeting, all the board members were chortling, slapping each other on the back, and toasting the future of the new Fubar Corp. And somewhere outside in the moonlight, floating on a nearby rooftop, Methane Mom smiled her big evil smile: another mission accomplished.

Methane Mom was the reason that Wendywoman could never hate any of corporate America's caustic characters. She knew where they had come from and who had been the source of all their *yesterdays*. Each was a brainwashed by-product, born out of a toxic corporate America, created by something far more evil than anyone could ever imagine. Since there was no one to die for their sins, it was up to Wendywoman to slice the umbilical cord and show them the way to a new *tomorrow*.

Methane Man had to go. He was the one caustic character for whom Wendywoman had zero sympathy. He was beyond rehabilitation. His *today* and *tomorrow* were driven by more than a screwed up *yesterday*; they were driven by a selfish, powerful urge to pollute every last inch of the working world for his own gains. For the time being, he was Wendywoman's most formidable foe.

Standing in the stairwell outside the CEO's suite, Wendywoman needed a change of her own. She'd been wearing the elevator operator uniform for too long now. Once she was properly attired in her superhero clothes, she powered up the greatest weapon in her Tote of Justice, the Executive Weed Whacker. She also had no choice but to surround herself with the Force Field from the MFHD. For what she was about to walk into, any type of emotional connection would be potentially lethal. Like a ghost buster, with her Executive Weed Whacker raised, she kicked open the stairwell door and burst through on Floor 8.0.

She was greeted by the sounds of a party behind the doors to the Executive Suite. There was loud music, whoops of victorious laughter that sounded like soldiers celebrating a successful ambush. Marsha's information had been spot on. The executives had gotten what they wanted, and as far as they were concerned, nobody else existed, so this was a victory. It didn't matter what happened to *other* people.

Wendywoman grabbed a handful of Executive Shush-up Biscuits for good measure and entered the suite. Champagne glasses shattered on the marble floor, and jaws dropped as the executives, who had felt invincible only moments before, saw the angriest, most determined superhero (who vaguely resembled that chick who ran the elevator but with a costume change) they'd ever encountered in their lives. Wendywoman unleashed the power of absolute realization and truth on a group of people who cowered in chronic memory loss and lies.

Zap! Pow! Zzztt!

The Venus Lie Trap sucked up denials, half-truths, justifications, and lies from every corner of the room. The executives' dropped jaws from the shock of her appearance made it easy for Wendywoman to hit most of the executives with a round of Shush-up Biscuits. Those who resisted, like Methane Man's number one lieutenant and yes-man, Not Me Lee, were taken out at the ankles by one perfectly aimed swipe of the Executive Weed Whacker.

Wendywoman looked around at the corporate carnage in the lobby of the CEO's suite. Unfortunately, Methane Man was nowhere to be found. Meanwhile, the Fubar CIO Box of Rocks Bill peered out from under a chair at Wendywoman.

"It didn't have to be this way, Bill. It still doesn't. You have a choice. Whether you like it or not, you are a role model for somebody, good or bad. You still have the chance to change your ways, disconnect from Methane Man, and possibly even inspire others," she told him.

He looked at her and then glanced toward the closed door of Methane Man's office. Wendywoman immediately knew that despite her best efforts, Bill's loyalties would always lie with the toxic pile of poop undoubtedly cowering behind the door. She switched her Executive Weed Whacker to high and kicked open the door. Methane Man had his back toward her. He was hunched over a wooden trunk in the corner of his office.

"What's the matter, Methane Man? Do you miss your mommy?" Wendywoman said, taking aim.

"Far from it, Elevator Girl." Methane Man sounded strangely calm, which slightly spooked her. Nevertheless, she kept her Executive Weed Whacker aimed at his head and circled around the desk to the corner to see what he was up to. Wendywoman looked into the trunk and gasped. It was filled with voodoo dolls, each a very lifelike resemblance of a different Fubar company employee. Traitor! Methane Man hadn't even spared his precious executives from his torturous wrath. Of course! He was loyal to no one except himself. Wendywoman was desperately trying to remain cool, but she was sick to her stomach at the sight of the voodoo dolls.

"Playing with your toys again?" Wendy jeered, trying to maintain control of the situation.

"You could say that." And very calmly, Methane Man stuck a sharp needle in Phrantic Phoebe's side. At that very moment, downstairs in the break room, where all the employees were still gathered, Phoebe grabbed her side, gasping, "No no no."

"Where did you get those?" Wendywoman demanded.

"They were a gift, from a woman who's like a mom to me." Methane Man sneered.

"So this is how she programs the caustic characters of corporate America," Wendywoman murmured.

"Exactly. And now I get to join in the fun." Methane Man turned to face her, holding up Maniacal Mean Marsha's doll. He had bound her arms and legs with twine to make her powerless. At that moment, back in her office, Marsha was reaching for the phone when her arm was suddenly yanked back to her side. She let out the furious screech of a captured animal.

"Stop that right now!" Wendywoman ordered, moving the Executive Weed Whacker even closer to his head, but Methane Man ignored her.

Squash! On Methane Man's desk, Leo's doll was crushed under the weight of a large rock engraved with the word "Force." At that moment, in the break room, Lame-O Leo sank down in his chair, hiding his head in his hands so nobody would look at him.

Next, the CEO reached into Sharkman Zak's cotton chest, pulled out his paper heart, ripped it in half, and put it back. At that moment, Zak reached into his back pocket for his wallet, took out a picture of himself with his ex-wife, and the son who had been number one in the exit line, and grabbed his own chest in emotional pain.

Methane Man used a penknife to slash open Serena's already blood-covered feet, using a red marker to create the fresh wounds. At that moment in the break room, Serena was walking back to the meeting from the snack machine when she cried out in pain and looked down at her feet, wondering where the fresh blood oozing through her nylon stockings was coming from. She had been walking through broken glass for ten years, seeing life only through her rose colored glasses, but this was a pain she could not ignore.

Still cowering under the chair in the CEO's lobby, Box of Rocks Bill suddenly forgot why he was there. Methane Man had just disposed of his little walnut brain in the wastebasket and then stuffed him in his back pocket for safekeeping. Bill looked up toward the door of Methane Man's office with a sudden desire to be closer to his boss.

The only doll that Methane Man spared from immediate harm was his fellow executive in crime, Not Me Lee. The CEO had wanted to test Lee's loyalty for some time now. There was something funny about that guy that he couldn't put his toxic finger on. It was as if he were exploring his other options. Methane Man slid a tiny noose around Not Me Lee's voodoo doll's neck—just enough rope to hang himself with if he strayed too far.

"You're not going to get away with this!" Wendywoman cried out, taking a swipe at Methane Man with her Executive Weed Whacker. He ducked, laughing and released a toxic cloud of methane gas into the room. Without the Force Field, Wendywoman likely would have passed out from the stench.

"And who's going to stop me? *You*—Elevator Girl—in that silly little costume with your gardening supplies? You have no power over me, or my creator, and you know it! You've always known it!" Methane Man said, rising from his desk to return to the trunk in the corner for more dolls.

"Methane Mom may have had power over me a long time ago, but not anymore. You know I decided to change my choices, so I could change my life," Wendywoman told him.

"Oh yes, because you—oh, special one—have *changed* your life and created a new *tomorrow* for yourself, right? Isn't that what you're always trying to get people to believe? That you're somehow different from the rest of us? That you're immune to all the evils of corporate America?"

"Nobody is immune to evil, not even me. The difference is, I make the choice to recognize it, confront it, and move in another direction," Wendywoman said.

Methane Man continued his insane rant. "Methane Mom created you just like she created everyone else. She wound you up and sent you into corporate America and made you successful. And how do you repay her? By turning your life around, and then—as if that wasn't bad enough—feeling like you need to be some *superhero* to all her other creations! That's some way to repay a favor."

"Methane Mom did not control me nor did she control my choices! Unlike you and your minions, *I take complete responsibility for my life*, Methane Man—the good, the bad, and the ugly. And you will never understand that!" she roared in a very un-Wendywoman manner.

Blood rose to Wendywoman's face immediately, and a level of fury she never knew existed within her came roaring out. She didn't really have a combat strategy to deal with Methane Man. After all, she hated fighting without purpose and preferred to use wisdom to settle the majority of the battles she got into. But this time, she knew she would be fighting for a reasonable cause: she had the rest of the Fubar employees to worry about. Plus, he really pissed her off. Let the *coup d'état* begin!

"I may not understand you or your kind," blustered Methane Man, while still shuffling through the trunk, "but one thing I do understand is how to stop you."

""What are you talking about?" she asked, and then she saw it.

Methane Man triumphantly held up a voodoo doll that looked exactly like her. "And if you think that gardening tool is somehow going to stop me from getting rid of you, once and for all, you've got another thought coming—you *drunk loser*," Methane Man sneered.

He was right too. As much as she hacked away at Methane Man with her Executive Weed Whacker, she kept missing over and over. For years she had been trying to defeat evil, and for years it had been eluding her. Now she watched in horror as he took her voodoo doll over to his wet bar in the corner, opened a bottle of vodka, and stuffed her inside.

The Executive Weed Whacker crashed to the floor of the office as Wendywoman grabbed at her neck, gasping for air. She was literally drowning in her *yesterday*. She fell to her knees as memories of her former self flooded in. Her lungs felt as if they were filling with the toxic, clear liquid. Wendywoman knew she was blacking out. He had won. Methane Mom had won again. Why had she ever thought she had the power to change anyone's *tomorrow* when, in this moment, it seemed she couldn't even change hers? Here she was, sliding back in time, farther and farther—drowning in her *yesterday*.

All the feelings she experienced while fighting to sober up, against what was often a crippling tide of fear, came crashing over her. Todd was always saying that you don't need a disability to be consumed by fear and ultimately stop functioning in your life. Lying on the floor of Methane Man's office, gasping for air and paralyzed with terror as image after image of the darkest times of her life flashed in front of her, Wendywoman understood Todd's words more than ever. As she slid further into her dark haze, she looked up and saw that the voodoo doll in her likeness had completely absorbed the vodka and was sinking silently to the bottom of the bottle.

"I will *not* sink to the bottom—not again!" The words popped into Wendywoman's brain like a bolt of lightning.

Just as she sucked in her last liquid breath, her outstretched hand closed around something—the Executive Weed Whacker. With her last ounce of strength, Wendywoman grabbed it and activated the one setting that Methane Man wasn't aware of—and had a deadly fear of. He had moved back into the corner, hovering over his trunk with his back to Wendywoman, certain of her impending demise. Feeling the sensation of heat on his back, Methane Man slowly turned around, right into a wall of *his* mortal enemy—*fire!*

He screamed as loud as he could, hoping it was loud enough for Methane Mom to hear him and save him. But he knew that cleansing fire was her enemy, too, and he was on his own. Wendywoman was back on her feet, breathing freely again but feeling buzzed. What the hell! She'd been a functioning alcoholic before (as if there really is such a thing), so even though it seemed like she couldn't go on, she knew she could. She had to! This needed to end quickly, before the warm feeling from the vodka became too much for her to resist. She tightened her arm muscles to steady the stream of fire shooting toward Methane Man from the end of her Executive

Weed Whacker. He flattened himself in the corner, trying to dodge the fire, knowing that just the tiniest lick of flame would instantly turn him into a human torch.

And then, the flames shifted. Satisfied that she had trapped Methane Man for the time being, Wendywoman directed her attention to her voodoo counterpart, still floating in the bottle of vodka. She grabbed the bottle and as Methane Man started to exclaim "Ha! I knew you haven't changed," Wendy surprised him by smashing the bottle in his wet bar. Then she extracted the doll from the wreckage and laid it on the counter. Her buzz immediately vanished!

"*Nooo!*" Methane Man yelled as Wendywoman aimed her Executive Weed Whacker at the doll, hit it with fire, and sent the doll up in alcohol-fueled flames—destroying it for good. "Now you and your mother have no more power over me. My life is completely my own," said Wendywoman, redirecting the Executive Weed Whacker, this time with the flames off, at Methane Man. She was satisfied that now that he knew about her ability to make fire, he would be a heck of a lot more obedient. Game over.

"You be a good boy now," she told him as she picked up the phone and called Todd for backup. She turned her back on Methane Man for only a split second, but in that brief moment he had reached into a closet, pulled out a golden parachute, and put it on.

"Oh no, you don't!" cried Wendywoman, once again aiming the Executive Weed Whacker at him. Methane Man immediately ran back into the corner, still wearing his parachute. "I am *not* going to let you do this again. You will not run out on this company just like you did the others, leaving us in this toxic mess you've created." Wendywoman told him firmly.

She briefly fantasized about what it would be like if this sort of "super-hero" confrontation could play out in every toxic CEO's office in corporate America. She knew that was the kind of fantasy that American office workers everywhere could enjoy. Her fantasy was interrupted by the sudden appearance of Tenacious Todd, who seemed only mildly surprised at the scene he walked in on.

"Wendy, way to go!" He smiled and gave her a pat on the back.

"Todd, I need another favor," she said. "I have to succeed today, no matter what it takes."

"And that means heading downstairs to the break room," her good friend finished her sentence.

"Exactly. And…" she started again.

"You need me to watch this guy and make sure he doesn't escape," said Todd.

"Think you can handle this bad boy?" Wendywoman asked, handing over her Executive Weed Whacker.

Todd eagerly took it in his hand with a huge grin on his face, like a kid who was just handed his very first Supersoaker Squirt Gun. "Oh, yeah!" he exclaimed. He pointed the tool at Methane Man, who looked slightly more terrified by the Executive Weed Whacker when it rested in Todd's single arm than he had when it was held by Wendywoman's two.

And with Methane Man under Todd's watchful eye and more-than-capable hand, Wendywoman headed out the door, down the stairs, and into the break room to complete her mission. She had cut off the monster's head. Now it was time to deal with its limbs, a group of wounded crabby crappy people who were unaware that their fearless leader was her hostage. How would they behave when they were free of Methane Man's toxic influence? Wendywoman was about to find out.

GATEWAY

ENTER   ELEVEN

http://bit.ly/wrO5HI

IN SUMMARY...

Now we've met the toxic head of Fubar up close and personal and the evil that created him and all the other crabby crappies that we all deal with every day—all around us and, despite our best intentions, very often in the mirror. With characters like this spreading their toxic gases from company to company, is it any wonder that corporate America is so fubar'd these days? Turn on the news any given day, and you'll see a Methane Man–type character grab his golden parachute, leave the mess he's created behind, and move onto his next target. How much more money can we print for these characters to burn through? If it's up to Wendywoman, she'll eventually get a chance to confront her real enemy—the elusive Methane Mom—and get some real answers.

Methane Man's Step: Those Crabby Crappy People You Call Friends

❖ The Wretchedly Unhappy Club.

- Are you a member? Are your friends members?

❖ Refine your inner circle. You become the company you keep.

- Release those who limit you, and connect with those who help you live more fully.

❖ Like it or not, you are a role model for somebody, good or bad.

- Who might you inspire today? Whose life might change because you smiled, said hello, or just provided a good set of ears and listened to what they had to say?

- With every act of kindness, you send a lifeline of love and hope to somebody who might need it today, and best of all, it's free. It costs you nothing to give, so there are no excuses.

❖ Nowadays we have to try harder because the pace at which we all move, combined with technology, isolates us from one another.

• The limited contact we do share becomes even more important.

CHAPTER 11

THE WATER COOLER

Wendywoman did not arrive at Fubar Corp. as a fresh-faced college graduate ready to take on the world like Serendipitous Serena. Nor did someone show up at her previous job with an open invitation like Mean Maniacal Marsha had done for Phrantic Phoebe. Nor did she float in by golden parachute like Methane Man. There was, however, one similarity between how she and the CEO were recruited: a secret meeting by a desperate board of directors looking for a way to pull its failing company out of a death spiral.

For Wendywoman, the challenge had all started exactly one year ago. The board had recently received the dismal results of the annual Fubar employee survey. The members sat there in their expensive, precisely tailored suits and passed the survey excerpts around the table. Each was worse than the last.

"Instead of actually learning how to do his job and fix the firewall, our dumb-as-a-box-of-rocks CIO just tells us what idiots we are for allowing viruses into the system. I've had it with this guy!"

"So let me get this straight: I bust my butt sixty hours a week trying to plug the money leaks that the CFO keeps creating, and it's somehow my fault that we're going broke?"

"Hiding in your office and pointing fingers at everyone else when his shit hits the fan is not my idea of an effective CEO."

"You call this leadership? A seeing eye dog could do a better job leading this company!"

It was during that meeting that one of the board members mentioned someone who was quickly earning a reputation in corporate America as a superhero of sorts, as someone who helped companies regain and retain their investments. Since that was about all the board members knew about this mystery woman, they naturally assumed that her greatest superhero power would be firing all the employees while avoiding any sort of workplace incident that would become breaking news on cable TV, saving them from having to do the actual firing. The first person on their termination wish list was the CEO who had duped them all during their last secret meeting.

So it was, that exactly 365 days before the firefight with Methane Man, on a morning when sunlight streamed in through the conference room windows, the mysterious corporate superhero who called herself Wendy sat at the head of the conference table, in the same seat where Methane Man had sat for his secret meeting. The board members studied her, trying to figure out what it was about her that the other companies who had recommended her were raving about. She certainly didn't look like the executive type. Rather than the MBA factory issue navy blue suit and closed-toe shoes, she had shown up in a red cashmere suit with a black ribbon tied around her waist and a lacy black camisole peeking out from beneath the jacket. Everything about her presence announced that they were either going to take her the way she was or not take her at all, that she wasn't changing for them. She'd been a rebel that way her entire career.

She smiled her mile-high smile, ready for whatever challenge was about to show up in her life. She loved a good challenge and loved the idea that in the months and years to come, she would have an opportunity to make a difference in the Fubar organization—as long as they all left her alone to work her Wendywoman magic.

Then, they got down to business, describing in detail how awful each individual Fubar employee was while passing pages of the employee survey down the table to her to make their point. When they finished, the board chairman folded his hands and looked her in the eye.

"So, Wendy, in light of all you've heard today, how quickly can you get rid of them?"

Wendy slowly finished reviewing the employee survey and looked at the board members with calm, steely resolve. "I'm not going to fire any of these people."

The board members registered shock, anger, and curiosity at the same time.

"What do you *mean* you're not going to fire these people? Why do you think we brought you here in the first place?" one of them asked her in stunned disbelief.

"My understanding," said Wendy, "is that you brought me in here to protect your investment by improving the morale, productivity, and profitability of this company. Correct? You want me to fix Fubar Corp."

"Well, yes, but, how else—I mean we've explored other options—you don't seem to understand that *nothing* works with these people. They're hopeless!" another board member exclaimed in frustration. Wendy desperately wanted to roll her eyes in disgust. These weren't board members; they were bored members. They took no real interest in any of the Fubar employees.

"Ladies and gentlemen, I have learned through my many experiences in situations just like this at companies just like this that *nobody* is hopeless, and there are always other options," explained Wendy.

"Look," said the chairman, "the only reason you're still sitting there and we haven't kicked you out is your reputation. Nevertheless, we're going to need to hear what you're planning on doing to get us out of this mess. The last guy who said he was going to fix everything just made everything a hell of a lot worse. We need some sort of assurance from you that this will be different."

"It will be very different. But I'm not going to fire any of these people. I'm going to change the people but not change the bodies. There's greatness in all people, and part of our jobs as leaders is to find it," said Wendy. "Real leaders find greatness in everybody. They don't just throw people out like disposable assets."

"That's all well and good, but what makes you think they're going to listen to you any more than they listen to anyone else? You think just because we give you the title of president and stick you in a nice office, they're going to automatically straighten up and fly right, just because *you believe in their greatness?*" another board member mocked.

Wendy smiled. "No, that's not what I think, and that's not how it will work," she said. "You can make me president if you want, but that's not how your employees will be introduced to me. That's not how they'll interact with me."

"Then how do you want to be introduced?" asked the chairman irritably, losing his patience with what he saw as a corporate psychobabble exercise by a woman who thought she knew everything.

"As the elevator operator," she told them.

It took a little more convincing, but the board's collective back was up against the wall, so they were ready to agree to pretty much anything at that point. The plan was put in motion: Wendywoman would go "undercover" at Fubar as the "elevator operator" to learn more about each Fubar employee— where they came from, what kind of toxic crap they were currently spewing to poison the company, and, most important, what needed to be done to inspire each one to reprogram a new *tomorrow*.

One of Wendy's conditions was that the board would allow her to do her job without interference or interruption. Well, at least for twelve months. Then, if she didn't get this mess turned around somehow, they could toss her out, too. In the end, they were so grateful that someone was promising to do something that they all agreed, though secretly they each feared that they were once more being taken in by yet a corporate con artist. But they did see the elevator operator plan as having a value-added bonus: the darn elevator was always broken anyway, and no repairperson in the city had seemed able to figure out how to keep it working. If this mystery woman wanted to play dress-up to fix the company, rehabilitate the employees, and fix the Fubar elevator all at the same time, they weren't about to get in her way.

When the meeting was over, Wendy shook hands with each of the board members, left the conference room, and retrieved a small red suitcase on wheels that she had left in the lobby with the secretary.

"Will you be needing a taxi back to the airport?" the secretary asked her, assuming that Wendy had failed to impress the board, as had the many others the board had recently met with.

"No, thank you. I'll just be heading down to the basement now to get my uniform," Wendy told the confused girl as she headed to the elevator, removing the "Out of Order" sign stuck on the door.

"That's out of…" the girl started.

"Order. I know." Wendy smiled and waved at the girl as she stepped into the elevator, which miraculously came to life. The secretary's chin dropped in awe.

Wendy took the elevator all the way to the basement without a single technical glitch. There, she found a brand new elevator operator's uniform hanging in a locker. The second hand on the clock on the wall moved to nine o'clock. A new day was about to begin at Fubar.

Now the last day of her contract was coming to an end. The sun was about to begin its daily kiss with the horizon. Wendywoman, who had changed in the stairwell back into her elevator operator uniform from her superhero duds, opened the door to the break room. She had left her Tote of Justice in the hall outside. Wendywoman knew that to get this group into the elevator and up to the roof, she would have to go in alone and unarmed. These people were already aiming enough weapons at themselves. It was her job to disarm them.

She walked in and surveyed the room. This was not the scared, angry mob that had tossed her on her head and chased her into the elevator earlier. This was a break room of broken, wounded souls.

She saw the results of Methane Man's voodoo magic everywhere. Serena had cut the feet off her nylon stockings and was tending to her bloody wounds with paper towels. Zak, who hadn't even noticed Wendywoman enter the room, was still staring sadly at the pictures in his wallet and rubbing his chest. Leo sat slumped like a rag doll in an orange plastic break room chair, staring at his hands. Phoebe held onto her side at the place where Methane Man had pierced her doll, wondering when the next stab of pain would hit.

They all looked at her, collectively remembering that she was the enemy. They were supposed to be mad at her, and plotting revenge against her, but none of them could remember why exactly. They weren't in the Memory Loss Lounge, but under the flickering buzz of the neon lights and in the midst of the acid smell of bad coffee in Styrofoam cups, none of them could put a finger on why they had such feelings of hatred—and fear—toward the elevator operator.

What, after all, had she actually done to them? The crabby crappies looked at each other for answers, but every face was blank, as if to say, "I don't know either, but I'm sure we're remembering this correctly."

The only caustic character missing from the room (other than Methane Man, of course) was Maniacal Mean Marsha, who was still hiding from her *yesterday* in her bleach-scented office upstairs. Even the executives with whom Wendywoman had just battled upstairs in the CEO suite, Box of Rocks Bill and Not Me Lee, had skulked into the break room, curious to see if the news of their victories had trickled down the ranks to the peasants. Since nobody was so much as glancing in their direction, where they stayed huddled like rats in the corner around the water cooler, they figured they were safe there for the moment—until Wendywoman came in. With the punishment that she had inflicted still fresh on their minds, the executives put their heads down and tried to merge with the walls. But then Not Me Lee pointed out in a hushed whisper that Wendywoman had switched back into her elevator operator uniform and was no longer wielding the gardening tool. This gave the executives the courage to at least lift their heads again.

"What did you do to him?" Not Me Lee asked Wendywoman.

The other wounded crabby crappies noticed the executives for the first time. Lee's question seemed to infuse a tiny shot of confidence into the rest of the room.

"What did I do to whom?" asked Wendywoman, stepping even further into the room.

"You know who, elevator operator. The CEO. You had no right doing what you did today. How dare you—a nothing, an uneducated nobody—threaten the head of this company!" Box of Rocks Bill chimed in.

"And what about Marsha? Whatever they're saying you did to the boss, did you do to her too?" asked Phrantic Phoebe. "I mean, where is she?"

"Since when are you worried about Marsha, Phoebe? And why on earth would the rest of you be concerned about Methane Man?" Wendywoman asked the room.

"Because they told us to wait here. Well, Marsha did, anyway, because the CEO trusted her to tell us. But we haven't seen either of them in awhile. We figure that you have something to do with it," Lame-O Leo said, lifting his head from his lap.

"I don't know where you get your information," Wendywoman said calmly, "but you have everything completely bass-ackwards. For your information, your fearless friend Marsha is hiding in her office upstairs, afraid of admitting the truth, which is that she has no real power at all. She has been fooling you for years, and you have gone along with it, assuming that for someone to act like that, she must be a powerful and important person. The only power Marsha has, though she's just now realizing, is the power to change the choices she makes to reprogram her future. That's the same power you have, and that's all I've been trying to make you realize. The reason you have been told to hate me, without realizing why, is that I represent making a powerful change so you can improve yourselves. Your friend Marsha just realized that today. And now I'm hoping each one of you will realize the same thing and make the choice *today* to accept change."

They looked doubtful, but they were listening. Even the executives huddled by the water cooler were paying attention. Wendywoman took that as an invitation to continue and drop another bombshell.

"And your feared and revered CEO? You're actually right on this assumption. I *did* do something to him. I kept him from doing further damage to all of you," said Wendywoman. "Do you know what he was planning to do? Did your friend Marsha tell you—or was I the only one she trusted with the truth?"

The executive huddle looked away and tried to climb into the walls again, as they knew exactly what was coming. None of the others answered her, so she continued. "All of you were about to lose your benefits. Well, not *all* of you, because a bunch of you were about to be fired. And the rest of you? Your friendly leader was going to leave you stranded here to pick up everyone else's workload with no benefits while he strapped on his golden parachute and moved on to the next company and his next group of suckers. Did you know that?"

Stunned silence, but like the calm before a storm.

"And," Wendywoman went on, as the executives in the corner gasped in terror at what was coming, "do you know who was to be spared this mistreatment? Do you know which Fubar employees get to keep their benefits and their jobs? Them!"

She pointed at Box of Rocks Bill and Not Me Lee in the corner, expecting a full-on mutiny. Sure enough, the tsunami came, but it wasn't directed at the cowards in the corner. The wave came at her instead. The broken, wounded group suddenly sprang to life, leaping from their chairs, jabbing their fingers at her, yelling, "You lie!" "You know nothing!" "…blah blah blah… just an elevator operator… blah blah blah!" "Liar!" Wendywoman stood her ground, letting them have their say with a neutral expression on her face. She knew she was looking at a group of very hurt, angry, betrayed people, and that none of it had anything to do with her. It was like a group of foster children all being abandoned by parents who they thought loved them, all at the same time. Wendywoman felt more empathy for each of them, in that moment, than ever before.

At the peak of their anger, the break room door suddenly opened and everyone stopped what they were saying, fingers in mid-jab. Maniacal Mean Marsha, still subdued by the effects of Wendywoman's visit, walked in quietly, somewhat trancelike after her traumatic, eye-opening day. All eyes in the room were on her, including those in the executive huddle. The executives crossed their fingers that Marsha would somehow follow through on the orders to do away with Wendywoman, as Methane Man had instructed.

It was not to be.

"She's right," said Marsha. "Everything she's saying is the truth." There was a collective gasp. If Marsha, the person who seemed to know about everything that happened at Fubar, believed the elevator operator's words, then they had to be true. Lame-O Leo, sensing a sea of change as his saboteur Not Me Lee cowered by the water cooler and his former tormentor Marsha, seemed to be a changed woman, found the courage to stand and seemingly take charge of the room. Wendywoman smiled with tremendous pride. She always knew he had it in him.

"So if we're to believe you, then Methane Man is no longer a threat to us. But what have you done to him?" Leo asked on behalf of the others.

"Tenacious Todd is keeping Methane Man in his office upstairs so he can't escape before you have a chance to confront him," Wendywoman said. She was pleased not to be interrupted by comments like "The one-armed guy?" Her characters were growing right in front of her. "Each of you deserves the chance to tell Methane Man how his actions have hurt you and others like you," Wendywoman continued. "None of you deserves to be stepped on and taken advantage of this way. To change your *tomorrow*, you must confront and release the things that are holding you back *today*—and Methane Man is one of those things. It's time for you to see his true colors, his true shades of mud."

The people in the room looked from Wendywoman to Marsha, seeking validation out of habit. Marsha nodded in agreement.

"It's time for your elevator ride upstairs," Wendywoman told them.

Each person knew what that meant by now. They knew now more than ever that there was a choice that awaited them on the roof. And they knew that it was inevitable. Some of them even looked forward to it, as a way of releasing the pain they were currently feeling as long as they were trapped in what they now realized was an extremely toxic *present*.

Led by less-lame-than-ever Lame-O Leo, they filed out of the break room and into the elevator. Wendywoman hung back and turned to the cowering executives in the corner. "You're invited, too. It's okay. I know it's not your fault, and the others do, too," she said kindly. "Why do you think they turned on me instead of you? This ride is for all of you just as much as it is for them." Keeping their eyes off her, the executives filed out of the break room and followed the others into the elevator. Last out of the room, Wendywoman shut off the flickering, buzzing neon lights. She'd always hated those things.

As the elevator rose up through the building without a single technical glitch or flicker of the toxicity indicator, the passengers inside were silent. It reminded Wendywoman of a SWAT team, quietly preparing to do battle with the bad guys. The elevator ride was fast and smooth: Floor 6.5, 7.5, 8.0… Wendywoman was relieved as they passed Methane Man's floor, believing that her trusted friend still had the situation well under control. Then, as they reached Floor 9.0, the Executive Suite, the elevator unexpectedly slowed. The passengers looked at each other in confusion.

"I thought we were going to the roof," Not Me Lee said, adding, "Only a few of us are even allowed in here"—just in case anyone had forgotten.

"Let's give it a try anyway, shall we?" Wendywoman asked cheerfully, motioning for everyone to exit the elevator. They all did, obediently gathering in front of the huge expensive doors.

"See? It's closed," said Not Me Lee, jabbing his finger at the sign on the door which read "Closed by order of the Fubar CEO until further notice" while jiggling the locked handles.

"Hmmm… you *might* be right, but I don't think so," Wendywoman said. "Excuse me, guys." She moved through the crowd to the doors, meanwhile pulling a shiny golden key from her pocket and—voila!—the Executive Suite / Memory Loss Lounge was open for business again. She held the doors open for everyone. "After you. Come on, don't be scared. Everyone's welcome."

One by one, and led by Lame-O Leo, the formerly caustic characters of Fubar filed into the formerly forbidden territory of the Executive Suite.

Chapter 12

The Executive Suite

OO**W**elcome to the Fubar Executive Suite. Soak it all in, folks, 'cuz it ain't gonna be like this forever!" That was it. The entire group decided that Wendywoman, the elevator operator, had completely lost her mind. First, she apparently assaulted all the company's executives. Then she revealed that her accomplice, the one-armed guy from Marketing, was at her behest holding the company's CEO captive at the end of a gardening tool. Now she had all but kidnapped them from the break room and talked them into some crazy "sunset elevator ride to the roof" where they were each going to have to make some big life-altering decision. But first, apparently, they had to join her while she strutted around the Executive Suite, which she had somehow opened with an actual key, even though only executives were allowed in and had keys.

The whole group of crabby crappies, even the executives who were used to the place, stood bunched together in the doorway, watching Wendywoman, who had a big goofy grin pasted across her face as she played tour guide. She gave specifics about the floor tiling, the Corinthian leather furniture, the chandeliers, and even the windowpanes. The group of characters at the door soon forgot the strangeness of the situation and began to follow Wendywoman around, looking where she pointed, and appreciating for the first time that a little bit of beauty actually existed at Fubar after all. Even the executives who were used to the room found things to admire that they had barely glanced at before.

"Why are you telling us all of this? I mean, yes, we appreciate the tour. But I thought we had to get to the roof?" interjected Lame-O Leo as Wendywoman led them toward a mysterious door in the corner hidden behind the shrubbery.

"What's this, a closet? A joke? I don't think Fubar has a president right now," said Box of Rocks Bill, gesturing towards the plain wooden door marked "President."

"Thanks for asking, Bill," Wendywoman continued, smiling like a kid with a secret. "This, ladies and gentlemen, is the president's office," she then announced.

"Yeah, Wendy, we got that much," snapped Marsha, showing a momentary flash of her "usual" self. But at least she had remembered Wendy's name, which was real progress.

It was time. Wendywoman clasped her hands together and began "the speech."

"Once upon a time there was a failing American company. The leadership was shitty, and everyone knows that shit trickles down from the top, right? Well, the company was able to stay afloat, barely, but then it started to sink quickly. The new owners and board of directors started bailing with the same old buckets they'd always used to try and save their investment. First they hired a CEO who, despite his many public scandals, convinced them that he could turn things around. But all he did was make the ship sink even faster, drowning a lot of good people. Finally, right at the point where they were considering bailing out themselves, the board of directors brought in a leadership expert, an experienced senior executive who had a proven track record of success in turning around companies just like this particular one. Her methods were a bit unorthodox, but her clients were always wowed by the results in the end. Yeah, she did piss some people off along the way. It took some time and effort on everyone's part, and some people leapt overboard because they didn't want to get with the program. Ultimately, though, this woman always salvaged the unsalvageable."

Wendywoman paused to let the group absorb her story. She noticed Phrantic Phoebe rolling her eyes.

"What's the matter, Phoebe?"

"That's the story of almost every company in America right now! They all think that bringing in this one person to fix everything will magically solve the problems. I've learned that there are just some things in this world that you can't control. They're just meant to be bad," said Phoebe.

"You're right," Wendywoman said simply.

"Which part is she right about?" Marsha demanded.

"That one person can't magically fix everyone else's problems. All each of us can do is create awareness of what's really going on and lead the way to something better. Phoebe's also right that there are some—actually a *lot*—of things in this world that you can't control. So why bother trying? People get laid off, benefits change, companies close. Take responsibility for yourself, and don't worry about things you can't control."

Wendywoman was sure she saw a flash of something in Phoebe's eyes. The others looked doubtful. "Here," Wendywoman said, rifling through her giant key ring. "Let me give you another example. Aha, there it is."

Click. The group watched in astonishment as the elevator operator unlocked yet another forbidden Fubar door.

"How is she doing this?" murmured a frustrated Box of Rocks Bill. He looked around guiltily as if expecting Methane Man or someone else to stop them at any moment.

"Oh, I'm sure it's fine," said Serendipitous Serena.

They entered the president's office and looked around.

"Do you guys know why I wanted to be president of *your* company?" she asked.

First there was silence. Then gasps. Then a chorus of comments: "Ohhhhhh… Wow… No wayyyyyyyy…" along with one lone, "I *knew* it!" from Lame-O Leo, who was gaining more confidence by the second. Wendywoman wondered if he was carrying his magic mirror or if the effects were becoming second nature to him.

"I came here to help because I *am* all of you. Actually, I *was* all of you at various points in my life." Wendywoman then gave the group abbreviated examples of how this was true—for example, there was the time just after she had sobered up when she was changing jobs because she hated one of the partners in the law firm where she worked. Being a practical joker, Wendy had wanted to leave her boss something special to remember her by so she had gone to a gag gift shop, purchased some fake dog poop, and left it in his briefcase. She later found out from a former colleague what a "shit storm" her little joke had caused at the firm. The gag poop looked so real that her boss had almost recreated the real thing in his pants. Wendy may not exactly have been Methane Man, but for a while, she left a trail of crap behind her wherever she went.

"To this day, I can emerge as any one of you on any given day. And it's not just me! Every single person out there, especially the ones roaming the halls of corporate America, at one point or another acts the way each of you does. That doesn't make all of them bad people, and it doesn't make you bad people either."

She looked around at their puzzled faces. "For ten years I crawled through broken glass because of my alcoholism," said Wendy, looking at Serena. "But that is part of my *yesterday*. I wouldn't change those ten years for anything or the additional nine years my transition took me from just being sober to being mentally and physically healthy. Those nineteen years have made me who I am."

Serena nodded, and Wendywoman could see that some of this was actually getting through, even past the rose-colored illusion of Serena's social media world. "I understand your *yesterdays*—what happened to each of you that you are holding onto *today*—because I lived them, in some way, shape, or form too. When I get tired or stressed out, my *yesterday* comes shining through. It's not like it goes away, like you can go to a Memory Loss Lounge and forget it. You have to transform it. I can't erase the fact that I drank a bottle of vodka every day, hurt people I didn't know, and lost my dad," she continued.

Wendywoman noticed Zak holding a picture from her desk that showed her with her kids. Zak was lost in thought. "Yeah, that's me. I have a real life just as you do. I'm not some genie in a bottle. I've made my mistakes too—big ones. But eventually I had to forgive myself for them and stop reliving the effects over and over." As she said this last part, she laid her hand over Zak's. He nodded and put the photo back down on her desk.

"It's about making sure you stay on track, and make different choices so you never completely go back to living trapped in that *yesterday*. Make the choice to carry your *yesterday* in a positive, not a negative, way. And most important, never assume that people know where you are coming from, just like you don't know where they're coming from."

"So that's why we're supposed to trust you, and let you lead us up to the roof to do—whatever—to us? Then what? You collect your paycheck and move onto your next charity case?" Not Me Lee cut in sarcastically. Wendywoman was pleased that many of the others glared at him.

"No. You each have to go up to the roof for your own reason. Even if it's just to see what else is out there and explore your horizons. You don't have to fly just yet but at least check out the airport," Wendywoman said.

Phoebe smiled; she actually freakin' smiled. The day was improving by the moment. Wendywoman smiled back.

"And by the way, you don't have to like me. You can even be angry at me as you have been for your own personal reasons, and now for being the new person in charge of this place. But I want you to know that no matter what is happening here, I won't give up on you. I haven't yet, right? That's because I get it. I was you, and I believe in you. I also remember the time in my life when I decided I was going to change. All your fears today about going up to the roof and making a decision? I've been there, too. I wouldn't ask you to do it if I hadn't already done it myself."

She gestured for the group to leave her office, locked it behind them and led them back toward the doors to the Executive Suite. "Something you should also know is that as of today, this beautiful room will no longer be the place where overpaid executives coasting on their boss's (or subordinates') coattails get to hide and forget the way they've treated people. The Executive Suite will no longer be a place to forget your *yesterdays*. The rugs will be removed, so you'll no longer be able to sweep your *yesterdays* under them. Your *yesterday* can be transformative if you choose and allow it to. This will be the place where that change is possible."

"What gives you the…" Box of Rocks Bill started, but then remembered that he was no longer speaking to the elevator operator anymore.

"Thank you for making my point, Bill. Yes, as you could probably tell from my tour, I have recently come to realize how special this room is. Too special, in fact, to be wasted for the kind of crabby crap that has festered here for years," said Wendy.

Marsha was making a polishing motion with her hand on one of the end tables. "It's time to make room for a new chapter at Fubar Corporation, and each of you has to decide whether you want to be a part of it or not. You can change, or you can leave, but it's your choice," Wendywoman announced.

Minutes later, after every last one of the group had piled into her elevator for the ride to the roof, Wendywoman locked the doors to what was once known as the Memory Loss Lounge and posted a new sign: "Corporate Therapy Lounge."

"By the way," Wendywoman asked as she got in the elevator and hit the "R" button, "What *were* you guys planning on doing to me anyway?"

They all looked at each other, and then at Marsha.

"I'm not really sure. We were waiting for Marsha to tell us," admitted Zak.

"I didn't know either," admitted Marsha. "I was waiting for Methane Man to tell me."

"Wow," said Wendywoman, "Toxic crap really does trickle down from the top doesn't it?"

"Yep," Lame-O Leo said confidently, looking over at Not Me Lee.

The elevator coasted to Floor R. "End of the line. Everybody out."

The group emerged like explorers out of a spaceship on a newly discovered alien planet. Up until then the roof was by far the most mysterious, forbidden, feared place in all of Fubar. Each character had his or her own illusions of what monsters might lay in wait on the roof. Was it a jungle? A futuristic city? A giant time machine?

Actually, it was, well, duh, the roof of an office building: flat, with air duct pillars here and there, and a concrete floor with a railing around the perimeter. No demons here. Wendywoman laughed at the mixture of confusion, disappointment, and residual anxiety on their faces. "What were you expecting? The bogeyman? He's down in his office, remember? And I'd be willing to bet that he put these ideas in your head about 'forbidden rooms' and things you should never ask about and just do because he told you to. Right?"

Most heads nodded. The executives, still loyal to their fallen leader, glared at Wendy. "Why would I bring you up here to intentionally harm you? After everything you know about me, don't you believe that I have your best interests in mind and Methane Man does not?" she asked the group.

"We'll believe it when we hear it from Methane Man," Marsha said, looking at Wendywoman defiantly.

"Ah, of course, Marsha. I would imagine this kind of sudden power shift does seem a little unbelievable to you, doesn't it?" Wendywoman asked.

She wasn't surprised at all that Marsha had shifted so quickly. Corporate therapy for caustic characters was a long process, and this was just the first step—rooting out the ones in the crowd who were willing to give it a shot. Everyone on this roof was exactly where he or she was supposed to be, including the defiant executives. Wendywoman still had yet to perform her first executive caustic character conversion at Fubar. Of course, the conversion was possible, but these days Methane Mom was spewing so many layers of crap all over corporate America that the executives who were mired and bound by it barely had an available window of "change" time before they became part of the problem themselves.

Now, it was time to bring out their leader and expose him for the coward he was. She walked back to the elevator, retrieving her MFHD from her Tote of Justice, and held it up to her mouth like a walkie-talkie. "Yeah, it's me. Bring him up, and bring the dolls," she said.

A couple floors down, with his ear pressed to walkie-talkie embedded in the handle of the Executive Weed Whacker, Tenacious Todd nodded. "You got it, Wendy." To Methane Man he said, "You, on your feet now. Move."

On the roof, the Fubar employees stepped back from the elevator in unison as if a slimy monster was about to emerge and attack them. Along with Wendywoman, they all watched as the outside floor indicator above them showed that the elevator was rising toward the roof.

CHAPTER 13

ROOF LEVEL

I t's hard to maintain your reputation as a menacing, intimidating, authority figure when you're standing there helplessly, sweating bullets and clutching a cache of voodoo dolls, while some one-armed guy from Marketing points a weed whacker at you and… well, sings the song he wrote for you.

In case you don't know me I'm Methane Man
If you're anywhere near you'd better turn on a fan
To repulse and offend I'll go to any length
Being a good guy has never been my strength
The man inside me is even worse
With my voodoo dolls I'll place on you a curse
Not a team player not one of the guys
I don't spread cheer I only spread lies.

As the elevator doors opened, the group of assembled employees took in the sight of the man who had caused them so much anxiety, sleepless nights, ulcers, and a sense of bitter hopelessness. Marsha looked particularly disheartened at the sight of the wizard being exposed as nothing but a big-mouth coward behind the curtain. Not Me Lee pulled out his pocket calculator and started punching in numbers to somehow make this whole thing compute. Sharkman Zak had a strange wry smile on his face. With the CEO's weakness exposed like this, there was just one word flashing in his mind: "promotion"! Serena suddenly felt all the pain in her feet from walking through glass for all those years and dropped to the floor to sit cross-legged. Phoebe was smiling… and murmuring, "Yes yes yes." Box of Rocks Bill was sweating and frantically looking for a way back to the Memory Loss Lounge to forget this day ever existed. He would break the doors down if he had to.

Lame-O Leo's day, however, had been improving from the moment Wendywoman had entered the break room. All the people who had made him feel worthless were crumbling. And on top of that, here he was on the roof—much higher than his tree house—and he was *fine*. He wished his father were alive to see.

"All right, you, out of the elevator, and don't try anything funny," Todd said sternly, although unable to control a little smirk at his new Dirty Harry role.

Still carrying his voodoo dolls, Methane Man pushed through the still-stunned group, grumbling something about elevator operators and one-armed human defects as his defense for the bizarre scene in which he was the victim instead of victor.

"Good, now we can get this whole thing straightened out and figure out what's what and who's the liar," said Not Me Lee. He was fighting for his normal world to return while simultaneously trying to clarify his own loyalties. Some of the things Wendywoman and Tenacious Todd were saying made a little too much sense for him. Nevertheless, he stood side by side with Methane Man as if addressing a company meeting as the CEO's right-hand man.

"We need some accountability here. The last thing we need is someone taking credit for something that someone else did. We've got this *woman* here saying she's our president and that we have to make some kind of decision to believe her lies or quit. This is preposterous! Now that our leader is here, it's time to separate the liars from the leaders," said Not Me Lee. He looked to Methane Man for some sort of validation.

"Well, what is it you want me to say anyway, you little butt kisser? You think the board tells me anything? My job is just to keep the place running, and if that means cutting a few jobs, a few perks… What do you people want from me, anyway?" Methane Man spouted angrily.

That clearly wasn't the answer Not Me Lee was looking for. The disappointment was obvious in his other loyal lieutenant as well. Box of Rocks Bill slid his hands into his pockets and tried to work out the details logically in his head, as to what was happening. Wendywoman was sure she saw a puff of ancient dust come out of his ears from the sudden activity between them.

"Are you telling us this madness is true?" Not Me Lee said, stubbornly clinging to his denial lifeline.

"I already *told* you people it was true—the layoffs, the benefit cuts, all of it. Do you people all have rocks for brains or something?" snapped Maniacal Mean Marsha, redirecting her betrayal in a familiar way with her back toward Methane Man, a leader she had trusted the most and gained power from up until earlier that day. "As to whether she's really the president, well, she does have a key to the office, now, doesn't she?" In Marsha's bureaucratic world, that was absolute validation.

"I don't understand why this is so shocking to you all. What kind of fantasy world are you all living in that you think working in corporate America is supposed to be rose-colored glasses and yes yes yes to all the money, happiness, and job security your stupid little hearts desire?" said Methane Man.

He dropped the voodoo dolls at his feet and placed his hands on his hips in an attempt to earn back some of the respect he imagined he had once had. Todd kept Wendywoman's Executive Weed Whacker pointed at the CEO's head as a reminder of how the tables had turned. Wendywoman stood in the back of the crowd letting it all play out. She'd already had her turn to speak. Now it was time to let Methane Man hang himself with his own words, just as he was trying to do to his loyal henchman Not Me Lee.

"Of course I was cutting benefits! Of course most of you were about to be fired! With the economy the way it is, what other choice did I have? Don't blame me! Write to Congress. And don't start muttering under your breath about trust, either. I'm sick of all the CEOs getting all the blame when we're just trying to make our companies profitable and keep the lights on in America. Sometimes that takes hard decisions, and it takes guts to make them. I'm not sorry for what I've done; I'm damn proud of it! If any of you were in my shoes, you wouldn't have the *guts* to do what I've done. I'm an L-E-A-D-E-R! Leader!" Methane Man spewed his garbage all over the roof.

He was doing exactly what other CEOs just like him did all over their roofs—spinning out the lies, hoping that enough innocent people would be duped so the CEOs could keep getting away with it over and over. He went on for a few more minutes, making his case with the usual illogical excuses that play out on the news every night. Then he stopped, folded his arms with a satisfied smirk, and looked around. He was certain that he had won this little battle, and that his loyal employees, the ones who had depended on him for everything for so long, would immediately come back to their senses and fulfill their job of destroying Wendywoman once and for all.

In the silence following his speech, though, the employees still seemed to be looking for more—more answers, more accountability, more honesty, more… something.

"Is that it? Is that all you have to say to us? After all you've done, all you've caused here over the years, all you were about to do to us… that's all you've got? 'I'm a great leader, and you people are weak'? Seriously?" Lame-O Leo spoke for the group.

"Of course, that's all he's got. That's all he's ever had, and I'm personally glad that Wendy has had the *courage*—more courage than this coward could ever understand—to tell you all the truth," said Todd.

"Thanks, Todd," Wendywoman said, walking around the edge of the group from the back to the front and standing next to Methane Man. "And now, it's time for each of you to make that decision we've been talking about today," she said.

The group squirmed and looked away.

"It's interesting, Lee, how you said that it's time to separate the liars from the leaders. From where I'm standing, we need to separate the leaders from the leapers. Which of you will decide that trying to change for the better isn't worth the trouble and time required and leave here? And which of you will stay, face your *yesterday*, and transform it into a brand-new *tomorrow* with endless possibilities?" Wendywoman asked, gesturing at the endless horizons that surrounded them on the roof.

"Hey! Get back here!" Todd yelled.

Methane Man had taken advantage of Todd's momentary distraction and was running toward the roof's edge, about to activate the golden parachute on his back. Wendywoman stayed put but yelled across the roof to the CEO.

"I'm surprised, Methane Man! I thought you'd at least want to stick around and find out who is truly loyal to you. Don't you want to find out who leaps with you? Won't that give you the peace of mind that you truly are the great leader you claim to be?"

Methane Man turned, considered her words for a moment, and strutted back to the group with a smile, though he kept his hand on the parachute's ripcord. "That's possibly the only intelligent thing I've ever heard you say," Methane Man said sarcastically.

She just nodded and returned her attention to the people who really mattered, the people she had a chance to help. She picked up the voodoo dolls and passed them out to their counterparts. They each stared down at their doll in awe, visibly making the connection to the wounds on the doll and the wounds they felt. Phoebe suddenly stopped fearing new pains in her side. Serena's feet felt better, and she stood up again. Zak placed his finger in the doll's chest where the heart should be. Leo straightened out his crushed doll. Marsha unbound the legs and arms of her doll. Lee quickly shoved his doll in his back pocket so he could kiss his own butt. Bill stuck his index finger through his doll's head, trying to figure out what was missing.

"If you want to go, then find your own way off this roof and back down to the place you're used to now. But if you want to stay, come over to the elevator where you can torch your voodoo doll, so nobody will be able to control you ever again. Then, your new journey toward redefining your *tomorrow* can begin," said Wendywoman.

"Wendy, wait. There's one more thing I have to do before they all make their decisions," said Todd. He walked over to a locked storage closet and came back with his keyboard and started to play the song he had promised Wendy earlier that day, which to her now seemed like years ago.

So your thinking life's a little rough
And it feels like a fight
So you're running, so you're searching
For that somewhere to hide
You're a wounded character in your own play
You wear a mask to hide the pain
Don't you think it's time to step into your own life?

You have the power to say, "I'll face my yesterday"
And find a better way

Yesterday today tomorrow it's all in your hands
Yesterday today tomorrow it's all part of the plan
The person you'll be is more than you were
Where's the future living in the past?
Yesterday today tomorrow it's time now my friend

Now you need to find your strength
To climb up the steps
Your non-toxic tomorrow is waiting for you now

You can't look forward if you're looking in the rearview mirror
What have you learned?
What road will you choose?
Can you be your own friend?

All the crabby crappies stood where they were, contemplating their individual decisions based on their individual *yesterdays*, *todays*, and what they were willing to risk for a better *tomorrow*. Methane Man once again took advantage of the mass distraction and headed for the ledge. This time, Wendywoman didn't try to stop him, and she motioned to Todd not to try either. It was Box of Rocks Bill who chased his corporate hero to the ledge.

"Wait! Don't forget me!" he gasped, grabbing onto Methane Man as he was about to take off in his golden parachute.

Methane Man gave a condescending chuckle and allowed his loyal lieutenant to latch on to the golden parachute that would bring them both to the next unsuspecting fubar-ish company.

Back in the circle, all eyes were on Not Me Lee, the other executive. Sensing his duty and unable to calculate an alternative, Lee walked slowly over to the ledge. Halfway there he turned to look at Wendywoman and Todd and momentarily considered changing his mind. Were these lunatics right? Was there a chance he could change his choices and his life and get out of this infuriating fog once and for all? He turned and took a step back toward the group. Just as quickly, Not Me Lee grabbed his neck, as if an invisible rope was pulling him back toward Methane Man. Once he got there, he hesitated, hovering next to Methane Man.

"Well, are you coming or not?" Methane Man snapped impatiently.

"I don't know," admitted Lee.

Methane Man and Box of Rocks Bill climbed up on the edge of the roof, ready to take off.

Zoooommmm!

Lame-O Leo was over to the ledge in a flash. "Well, *I* do!" said Leo as he pushed his double-crossing boss, Not Me Lee, onto Methane Man just as the parachute lifted off. Not Me Lee was relieved. Once again, another important decision had been made for him. His conscience felt lighter than it had for months.

The extra weight was too much for the golden parachute, though, and the three toxic executive leapers started a twisting spiral downward. The other characters rushed to the ledge to watch, anticipating a corporate splatter on the pavement below.

Wendywoman, however, was looking up, not down. What had been a fairly cloudless, sunny sky was now filling with billowing, dark, ominous clouds overhead. She knew what was about to happen a split second before it did, and looked at the surrounding roofs for the mother of all caustic characters. Wendywoman knew she was nearby. This wasn't the kind of show she missed.

The plummeting executives in their tangled golden parachute were only moments from doom, when… *Zap!* A tremendous bolt of lightning came out of the dark clouds, instantly untangling the parachute and sending it floating into the air higher and higher, until it disappeared completely with its toxic cargo into the horizon. The sky immediately cleared, the sun emerged brighter than ever, and a rainbow appeared overhead.

The group exchanged amazed murmurs. For those left on the roof, the decision was now clear. One by one, led by Lame-O Leo (with the biggest grin on his face yet!), each formerly crabby crappy filed over to the elevator with his or her voodoo doll, picked up the Executive Weed Whacker, torched the doll, and got into the elevator to wait for the next step of the journey.

While everyone boarded the elevator, Wendywoman waited for Todd, who was stowing his keyboard in the storage closet. She waited for him to join her, but he just stood smiling at her.

"Come on, slowpoke. Time for our next mission," she teased.

"Did I ever tell you about one of my first challenges after my surgery?" he asked from over by the closet.

"What? What are you talking about?" Wendy asked in confusion, standing by the elevator with her impatient load of characters.

"It was brushing my teeth. Not the brushing part, but the putting the toothpaste on the toothbrush part. Half the time the toothbrush would fall over on the counter or onto the floor, and the toothpaste would no longer be on the brush." he laughed.

Still trying to figure out where on earth her friend was going with this, Wendy walked slowly over.

"So, my choice was either not ever to brush my teeth again or figure out a way. Did you know they make square toothbrushes that stay flat on the counter? Or that you can hold a toothbrush in your mouth backwards and put toothpaste on the end like lighting a cigar? Because the most obvious way of doing something was taken away from me, I learned a lot of other ways of doing the same thing. Suddenly I found out all these other choices I had that I never knew about," said Todd.

Wendy wasn't stupid—far from it. She knew Todd well enough to know he was trying to tell her something. She stood quietly, fighting every urge to interrupt, and let him continue.

"It's such a big part of life—learning to deal with your choices and challenges, learning to love where you're at in life, and choosing to be okay with it. I know you get that more than anybody, Wendy. I mean, it took you nine years after you sobered up to work through your nine steps in order to build equity in your life. You've lost your job a couple of times, been divorced, and faced major health challenges along the way. Yet you kept pushing forward, investing in yourself, and seeking out new challenges. And Wendy, you've always inspired me to do the same for myself. Which is why…"

Wendy couldn't keep her mouth shut for any longer.

"Is this about our kiss?" she blurted out. "Because I'm so sorry, Todd! I never would want anything to ruin our friendship and—"

Todd laughed and put his arm around her shoulder.

"No, Wendy, this is not about our kiss. I *loved* that you did that. I know that it was a reflection of our deep, wonderful friendship, and I feel exactly the same way about you. I'm not leaving because of that. Not at all," he told her.

He'd said it. He was leaving here. It was official. Wendy sighed. She had known it was coming. She knew that Todd would, and should, eventually spread his enormously talented wings and fly as high as she knew he could. Even so, she felt the pangs of loss for this phase of their friendship. But she nodded anyway, forcing a brave smile.

"I do get it. We've gone as far as we can here together," she said.

"Yes. But you know I'll be around now and then and anytime you need me," he said.

They both laughed. Of course they would be there for each other. They laughed like two hysterical idiots until tears started rolling down their faces.

"Hey! You wanna wrap it up out there, lovebirds?" Marsha screeched across the roof. Oddly, she seemed ready to laugh as well.

Wendy and Todd wiped their faces and fought to breathe. "Of *all* the people who can't wait for corporate therapy!" she gasped, still laughing and gesturing toward Marsha.

"Seriously!" Todd responded.

"Let me guess, you're going to go become a test pilot for the government," Wendy teased.

"Yeah, exactly. No, it's always been about the music for me and always will be. Gotta give it a shot. In fact, I just got a gig touring with a Christian rock band. I leave Thursday," said Todd.

"*You* are going to be unbelievable," Wendy told him. She followed Todd toward the staircase. "Steps as always."

"Yup. Gotta do the steps," he said. And then, with his usual wave and sparkling smile… "Bye, Wendy! See you later."

Tenacious Todd had left the building. Wendywoman sighed and turned back to the Fubar characters waiting for her in the elevator. This mission was over, and she deemed it a success. She'd never expected Box of Rocks Bill or Not Me Lee to change their corporate colors. The fact that everyone else was willing to try, even Maniacal Mean Marsha, gave Wendywoman hope for all companies.

Yes, her mission had done some good today, but she knew that corporate America remained toxic with evil lurking around every water cooler. As Wendywoman crossed the roof back to the elevator, she felt one set of eyes boring into her from afar—a presence on a rooftop somewhere nearby proved her point. Evil was lurking everywhere in business, and its source, Methane

Mom, was watching Wendywoman's every move, biding her time, and battling to stay one step ahead of the good Wendywoman was doing.

Nobody can rid the world of all its caustic characters in one foul swoop—not even a superhero with a Tote of Justice filled with weapons. In reality, every company needs its version of Wendywoman. Every single person has the choice to make it a personal mission to stop complaining about the leaders, stop waiting for the boss to get better, and become a leader in their own life. People can make these changes for themselves.

The elevator doors closed, and Wendywoman pressed the button that used to be for the Executive Suite/Memory Loss Lounge. It would now take them to the Corporate Therapy Lounge. The easy part was revealing the people who want to change versus the ones who are not willing. Now, thought Wendy, the hard work begins. She would have to teach them all how to grow a PAIR by learning the true meanings of power, autonomy, intimacy, and reciprocity, if they were to have any chance of resuscitating Fubar Corporation.

CONCLUSION

STEP BY STEP

Why hat have we learned from this superhero tale of Wendywoman and her caustic corporate characters? Did you recognize any of the Fubar characters from your own experiences at work? How did you deal with them as opposed to how Wendywoman did? Wendywoman's Tote of Justice is a feat of magic, of course, but the intended effects of each tool can be replicated by your behavior and choices in real life. Most everything in life has a dual purpose: It can be either a weapon or a tool.

For example, water can hydrate you, but you can also drown in it. A hammer can build things, but you can smash your hand with it. The real trick is to take a look at everything at your disposal, and see how you can turn them into tools. Those things woven throughout your life that seem like weapons— some of them causing destruction—may be able to provide you with some lessons that help instead of hurt when viewed from a different perspective.

The reason I brought these characters together in a very personal way is that they represent me—and you—on any given day. In the playground of life, when do your inner crabby crappies show up? When you're tired and cranky, does Marsha suddenly join the party? When you just can't take any more bad news, do you don Serena's rose-colored glasses? Do you sometimes have trouble forgiving yourself for a mistake, and so, like Zak, decide it's easier to take your pain out on others? Or maybe you work with the public on a daily basis, and find that after your last button has been pushed, telling everyone "no" requires a lot less effort than saying "yes" and going the extra mile for them.

It's okay to admit that you frequently become the characters in this story. As Wendywoman told them in the Executive Suite, it doesn't make you a bad person. The difference between our *yesterdays*, when we played these characters without realizing it, and our *today* and *tomorrow*, is that now we can see them coming, and when they act out, we can apologize for their behavior and vow to do better.

As much as I hope you enjoyed and even got a few laughs from the fantastical tale of Wendywoman, her dear friend and personal inspiration Tenacious Todd, and the crabby crappy people of Fubar, it's these simple nine steps woven into the story that I want you to learn and apply in your own life. Here they are, uncut, unplugged, and ready for immediate use.

Step 1: Change Your Choices, Change Your Life

It's never too late to change your choices and thereby change your life. Everyone has a shot at creating the life he or she wants, no matter what the circumstance. Make a decision *today* that is different from *yesterday*. Self-awareness is your number one priority.

If you don't like your life, it's relative to the bad choices you've made. Have you created an "alibi" for your life? Who has been the face of the blame? Take just one bad choice you have made in the past. Peel away the layers, and gain a valuable perspective on where the responsibilities lie. Be honest.

You can talk yourself into or out of almost any situation, good or bad. This is all about setting a positive path and attaching emotion to it. The same level of hysteria applied to a negative situation can be applied to a future goal or objective before it actually happens. Just setting the goal is not enough.

Slam the door of your mind shut to negative thoughts, so that the windows of opportunity may open for you. Sometimes you have to know what you don't want in order to know what you do want. Negative events are uncontrollable; negative thoughts are not. In order to have complete control of your emotional state, you must give power to your feelings. Let the bad ones go.

Don't neglect the journey; traveling with hope is sometimes better than the arrival at your final destination. Appreciate your personal circumstance. If you allow hope and fear to travel together, the journey will not fulfill you. Be grateful that you own the choices along the way. Happiness doesn't hide in a new house, new career, new friend, and it is not for sale. If you cannot find contentment in yourself, you will never find it elsewhere.

Step 2: Stop Living Life on Autopilot

Are you living a shrunken little life? Get out of your own way. Give your life permission to expand. We keep our lives restricted by doing the same things day in and day out. The gap between here and there is not as big as you think.

Stop standing on what was, or even what is! Use the past to propel you forward, not to pull you back. You must understand that change is positive and part of who you are. Exercise change daily. Make your comfort zone off limits.

Most of us love to cling to what we know—what we are comfortable with—and are quick to debate our position if someone suggests a different way. There is a tendency to go on believing what we have always believed, all the while trying to have a different life experience. This may explain your stagnant life. Throw your daily routines out the window, try something new, and surprise yourself.

If it doesn't work—if it's broken—fix it! If it's not broken—fix it anyway! Don't trick yourself into thinking that something is working, so you shouldn't change it. By the time you have figured out that it isn't working, it will be too late. Make a habit of finding things that are working in your life, and make them better.

Transformation is a constant in life, whether you want it or not. Rather than forcibly resisting the new, welcome change, and call it good. Take every risk and embrace every opportunity to provide a better life for yourself. Every day new cells are born and old cells die. Your body is constantly in a state of change. Match up your external environment and embrace the evolution. Be born into the parts of your "unlived" life.

Step 3: You Are Your Most Valuable Asset

Invest in yourself by believing in yourself. Don't wait for a boss, a teacher, or someone else to invest in you. The only person signed up for that job in this lifetime is you. If you can't believe in yourself, why should anyone else? If you depend on things outside of yourself to supply you with joy, you will be doomed to disappointment.

Peel off and discard any labels others have felt compelled to stick on you. Is your wardrobe filled with labels and lies that others have taken upon themselves to give to you? If so, it's time to clean out your closet and reveal the truth. Only you know who you are.

Never listen to anyone who tells you what you can't and shouldn't do. How do they know? They are not you. Heeding their advice will only result in disappointment. Be the leader in your own life.

You are on your own in this world—it's your responsibility to save yourself. No one will throw you a life preserver; you must learn to swim. Avoid scenarios that create judgment and self-doubt. It is your job to release others from this responsibility. Life is for living on your terms, not theirs.

Don't just do the right things for your life—do them faster, better, and more often. What are you waiting for?

Step 4: Always Go the Extra Mile

Who's watching you? You will never reach great heights of success if you perform at high levels only when others are watching you.

Sometimes, when it is not your job to do it, it is a once-in-a-lifetime opportunity to prove that you can. Participation and cooperation over and above what's expected create enduring power, whereas forced participation and cooperation will end in failure.

Always do your personal best. Only you know what that is. Learn to dismiss your tendency to believe first impressions or make quick judgment calls. Liking or disliking someone is a choice. Don't make that choice until you have all the facts. You never know if what you are experiencing is an individual's personal best at that moment in that circumstance.

Work to your highest standards. Attitude + Quality of Service + Quantity of Service = The Job You Hold. Excel in all three, and the promotions will take care of themselves. If you want the shackles to fall off, throw yourself into your work with enthusiasm and with initiative.

Don't get caught up in the cycle of trying to figure out why somebody did something or questioning a particular circumstance. The path that speeds us toward our dreams and desires is filled with detours and potholes.

To the degree that you go the extra mile, your life can be equally fulfilling and satisfying. If you don't, the only person you will hurt is yourself. Mediocrity in the workplace creates insecurity: going the extra mile doesn't guarantee that you won't be downsized, but being mediocre certainly does (at some point).

Step 5: The Secret Power of Serendipity

Yes, crappy things happen to good people. Life is a series of problems. You are either in one now, just coming out of one, or getting ready to embark on another. Our job is not to ignore difficult or painful situations, but to acknowledge them, learn from them, forgive ourselves for getting into them, forgive those we believe contributed to them, and then release them.

How we think and respond can be more dangerous than any adversity we face. The greatest challenge in life is to control the process of our thinking. Don't allow outside forces to initiate action in your life. See yourself as the initiator of direct action.

Train yourself from this moment on to appreciate and find happiness in the simplest of situations. Start small and change the fabric of your thinking. This will manifest itself in all situations. Change direction rapidly and come up with different, creative ways of responding to challenges.

The path is never clear. Your view of the world will have a strong influence on your actions. The same external event can be viewed, reacted to, and judged differently from a different perspective. In the words of Winston Churchill, "When going through hell, keep going." Life is the perfect teacher.

Step 6: Invite Discipline into Your Life

Sloppiness in life allows more variables to creep in and spoil your plans. Tighten up! Identify the things that *you* can control.

Failure is a few errors in judgment repeated every day. Failure doesn't happen overnight. Don't believe in or settle for failure.

Stop stressing over things you can't control. Lighten up! Release all things where you have no impact.

Play to win? Sure, but lose like a champion. Failures and losses are all part of success. Make each loss a useful gain for growth and change

Step 7: Living Your Life in the Exit Line

Time is the great equalizer. Make time for what you love. Don't take things personally.

Will you live before you die? Make your life the priority; everything else is secondary. Have the courage to use your voice to send your desires into the world.

Our natural inclination is to judge people. Don't waste precious moments spending your time labeling anyone: stylish, sloppy, pretty, too thin, too fat, too old, too busy. Celebrate your individuality. Be comfortable in your own skin. Have you ever judged someone negatively only to later have that person become a good friend? If so, you have personally experienced the perils of the judgment cycle.

Learn how to dismiss your natural tendency to believe your first impressions. It is a complete waste of time—the one thing you can't get an accurate read on. Try and understand that everyone has a yesterday. Liking or disliking someone is a choice.

Step 8: Power versus Force

Everybody is made of the same stuff; it is what you do with your stuff that matters. "Stuff" is like electricity: it can light up a room or electrocute someone. Most people rarely give thought to how their words or deeds impact others.

Stop and ask yourself: Do those who walk away after meeting me feel appreciated, inspired, respected? Do they feel liked? Remember: You may think you are a good person deep down, but it is your external landscape, not your blissful inner landscape, that most people can see.

Words can be dangerous weapons because you can't take them back. Physical wounds can often heal quickly, but emotional wounds linger and sometimes never heal. There are no degrees of honesty, only absolutes. Either you are honest or you are not. If you cannot be truthful in what you say and be loving in how you say it, don't say anything at all.

Delivery is worth more than the words you speak. Bad information delivered the right way will get you farther than good information delivered the wrong way. Are you someone who lights up the room or darkens the doorway?

Step 9: Those Crabby, Crappy People You Call Friends

The Wretchedly Unhappy Club. Are you a member? Are your friends members? Refine your inner circle. You become the company you keep. Release those who limit you, and connect with those who help you live more fully.

Like it or not, you are a role model for somebody, good or bad. Who might you inspire *today*? Whose life might change because you smiled, said hello, or just provided a good set of ears and listened to what they had to say? With every act of kindness, you send a lifeline of love and hope to somebody who might need it *today*, and best of all, it's free. It costs you nothing to give, so there are no excuses.

Nowadays we have to try harder because the pace at which we all move, combined with technology, isolates us from one another. The limited contact we do share becomes even more important.

GATEWAY

ENTER

THIRTEEN

http://bit.ly/yUWR8p

AFTERWORD

OUT OF THE BASEMENT

I t was years ago on a Sunday morning when the sound of the alarm buzzer was playing over and over. I finally reached over to shut it off. Oh shit. It felt like I got hit in the head with a baseball bat—again. Despite the fact that I had repeatedly vowed not to let this happen, it was another one of *those* nights, and of course, I couldn't remember why my damn head hurt worse than normal—well, as normal as it could be for me. As I rolled over to get up, I stared at my pillowcase. What was that? Without my glasses, it looked like blood. What the hell was going on? *Bang, bang, bang.* It felt like a freight train was plowing through my head. I threw my legs over the side of the bed and closed my eyes to get my bearings. Whooooo! What had happened last night?

I grabbed my glasses off the nightstand and stumbled into the kitchen, or more accurately, into a Manson-esque scene of *Helter Skelter.* Oh my god! Bloody handprints on the fridge, furniture, and walls, droplets of blood dripping from the counter, and fresh bloodstains everywhere. Who got killed in the kitchen last night? Where was my roommate, Katie?

Halfway back down the hallway, searching for a body, I caught a glimpse of myself in a mirror. I stopped, froze, and looked at the woman who stared back at me. Huh? The top of my head was shaved, and a thick row of surgical stitches formed a train track across the top. Had I been scalped? For a moment, it was all about me, and then I broke into a cold sweat as the horror set in. I ran to the window to see if my car was in the yard. Yep. No police in the driveway. Still in bare feet and pajamas, out the door I went to inspect, even if I didn't know exactly what was I looking for. I was clearly injured, but had I injured anyone else along with me? A quick trip around the car revealed nothing. I exhaled a big sigh of relief. If I had hit someone, something, there would be evidence, right? A bump, a dent, or worse yet, blood. Besides the obvious stitches in my head, there wasn't a single clue that anything had gone wrong last night. God must have been with me again.

Still having no idea about anything except the fact that it was a Sunday morning and I was expected at church, I got cleaned up, swallowed lots of aspirin, donned my favorite hat to hide the bad hair day, and headed off to church. Good thing I didn't get pulled over on the way. I most definitely would have gotten a morning-after DUI. My mom's friends Pat and John accosted me the moment I arrived.

"How are you? Are you okay? We didn't expect to see you this morning."

Since I was looking perplexed, they filled me in on the details of my Saturday night.

I am a great cook. So naturally, my church had put me in charge of its annual apple festival. I celebrated the honor by drinking all day and into the night, while carrying out my apple festival duties.

That night, Pat and John caught me, keys in hand, on my way to my car and fortunately had the good sense to take my keys and drive me home. John drove my car home, and Pat followed along, with me dozing in the front seat.

"Are you okay?" Pat had asked with great concern as she let me out in front of my house.

"I'm fiiiinnnne," I said, channeling my inner Serena.

"Are you sure you're okay?" she asked again as I planted my feet on the driveway, getting out of the car.

"I'm fiiinnnne."

John had just parked my car in the backyard and was heading down the driveway as I was heading for the side door. He watched as, in seemingly slow motion, the disaster unfolded. While fumbling for my house keys and simultaneously trying to keep my balance, I tripped, spun around backwards, and fell flat on my back. Unfortunately, on the way down, my head had a meeting with the corner of the concrete landscaping bricks. The three inch slice in the top of my head bled profusely. But I was "fiiiine." *Just let me in the house to go to bed, and I'll be fiiiine.* As I pressed my hands to my head and then to the door, the counter, the refrigerator, the blood kept coming, and Pat and John were convinced that I was not fine. Off to Marymount Hospital we went.

Pat and John told me that the doctor said I was too bombed for anesthesia to be safe. The twenty-plus stitches would have to be handled without it. I was not a happy camper. He also said that if the gash on my head had been a quarter-inch deeper, I'd have moved right to the front of the exit line and died. As it was, I was pretty darn close to the front.

I was a quarter-inch from missing my destiny to be a self-appointed corporate crusader and make a difference in people's lives. I was a quarter-inch from watching my kids grow up and being their mother. Each day that I was drinking and getting myself into situations like this, and the one at the beginning of the book in the basement, I was moving closer and closer to the front of the exit line. Thankfully, after one dreadful weekend in July 1986, I ended up in an outpatient rehab program for thirty days, which was the beginning of my new life.

You hear it all the time: I'm going to start working out tomorrow. I'm going to start that diet tomorrow. I'm going to pursue my passion tomorrow. I'm going to take that vacation tomorrow. I'm going to spend more time with my family tomorrow. I'm going to change my life tomorrow. But the exit line does not offer precise little numbers like the ones you pull out of the machine at the deli to indicate when your number will be called.

You've just read the tale of a bunch of crabby crappy people who were hopelessly mired in their traumatic *yesterdays* that they allowed to dictate their toxic *todays*; the idea of changing their *tomorrows* for the better—the idea of the dreaded "roof"—left them cowering under buzzing, blinding neon lights on ugly plastic furniture in a break room, awaiting further instruction from a boss they all *hated* and didn't trust. And until they saw that roof for themselves and saw that it was just an ordinary roof, that the extraordinary decision would have to come from within them, they each thought that *tomorrow* was an abstract metaphor for something that could never exist for them.

When will your *tomorrow* start? When will you make the decision to take the elevator ride to the roof, as much as it scares you and as much as other people are trying to convince you to stay in the break room and Memory Loss

Lounge? Look at the world around us! There is no time to waste. *This* is the time to change your life.

I recently found myself on the other side of town. I had taken a wrong turn and got lost on the way to an appointment with a new client. Damn GPS! Before I knew it, I was standing in front of that mysterious building with the basement I had woken up in that morning years ago, the morning I came to on the cement floor alongside a couple of empty bottles, broken shoes, and no memory of how I got there. I spotted the door to the basement where I had emerged blinking into the sunlight that day, frantically wondering how I would get back to a job and a boss that I hated.

I couldn't help myself. I wanted to see it again. I wanted to see if it was the way I remembered, or if the whole thing had been a dream. But the door was locked. Apparently this was an "out" door only. I considered looking for another way in but thought better of it. I'd been there before, and it had taken me this long to figure a way out. The last thing I needed was to retrace my steps.

Walking away from that building, I realized that, yes, once in a while I would take a wrong turn and end up lost in my *yesterday*. But that didn't mean I needed to stay on the same path and become hopelessly lost. The basement would always be there, and maybe I'd even end up in it once in a while. But the difference between my *yesterday* and my *today* is that I had now mastered the steps to get out of the basement and on with my *tomorrow*.

GATEWAY

http://bit.ly/wxSfku

CPSIA information can be obtained at www.ICGtesting.com
Printed in the USA
LVOW041534090512

281056LV00002B/18/P